THE
DIRECT LINE

THE
DIRECT LINE

AN OFFICIAL
NIGHTINGALE CONANT
PUBLICATION

SOUND WISDOM
P.O. Box 310
Shippensburg, PA 17257-0310

For more information on publishing and distribution rights, call 717-530-2122 or info@soundwisdom.com.

Quantity Sales. Special discounts are available on quantity purchases by corporations, associations, and others. For details, contact the Sales Department at Sound Wisdom.

While efforts have been made to verify information contained in this publication, neither the author nor the publisher assumes any responsibility for errors, inaccuracies, or omissions.

While this publication is chock-full of useful, practical information, it is not intended to be legal or accounting advice. All readers are advised to seek competent lawyers and accountants to follow laws and regulations that may apply to specific situations.

The reader of this publication assumes responsibility for the use of the information. The author and publisher assume no responsibility or liability whatsoever on the behalf of the reader of this publication.

ISBN 13: 978-1-64095-040-5
ISBN 13 Ebook: 978-1-64095-041-2

For Worldwide Distribution, Printed in the U.S.A.
1 2 3 4 5 6 7 8 / 22 21 20 19 18

Cover design by Eileen Rockwell
Interior design by Susan Ramundo

CONTENTS

INTRODUCTION

Raised during the Great Depression, Earl Nightingale (1921–1989) was from a young age invested in the pursuit of knowledge, keenly desiring to understand what enabled some people, especially those born without special privileges, to reach their goals while others did not. Like Napoleon Hill, he dedicated his life to studying success—what it entailed and how to obtain it—and became in the process one of the leading authorities on what makes people successful.

After serving in the Marine Corps, Nightingale built a career in network radio, hosting his own daily commentary program on WGN. Despite making enough money from commission on the program's advertising sales that he could have retired at the age of thirty-five, he decided to purchase an insurance company, spending a significant amount of time motivating its sales force to achieve greatness. Because of his effectiveness in encouraging his employees, one of his sales managers suggested that he record his advice—an idea that resulted in *The Strangest Secret*, the first spoken word message to win a Gold Record by selling over a million copies. Then, in 1960, together with Lloyd Conant he cofounded Nightingale Conant, an electronic publishing company that became a world leader in personal development.

Nightingale and Conant also worked together to produce a daily radio program called *Our Changing World*, which became one of the longest-running, most widely syndicated radio shows in history.

Often called the "Dean of Personal Development," Nightingale broadcast his radio programs for more than three decades on over 1,000 radio stations in twelve countries around the world, making him one of the most listened-to broadcasters in history. An inductee into both the Radio Hall of Fame and the International Speakers Hall of Fame and a winner of the prestigious Golden Gavel Award, he dedicated his life to helping others achieve personal success. In *Direct Line*, Nightingale presents a collection of his most valuable insights into achieving real and lasting success in one's career, relationships, and finances. The messages shared in it have helped countless listeners begin the most exciting and rewarding journey on earth—their journey of self-discovery and personal fulfillment. Collected, transcribed, edited, and presented for the first time in print, these messages can help you take control of your life and find happiness and contentment from the journey of striving toward your goals and cultivating a meaningful existence.

At the beginning of the program, Nightingale explains that "the purpose of *Direct Line* is to explore ideas—the best ideas from the past and present as they pertain to you and me and the mystery of our lives—and to discover why people do the things they do and why they don't do some of the things they could do; why they live the way they do, believe the way they do, and work and play the way they do." Drawing on the wisdom of the world's greatest thinkers—everyone from the great philosopher Plato to nineteenth-century transcendentalists like Ralph Waldo

Emerson and Henry David Thoreau, to psychologists such as Abraham Maslow and Carl Rogers, to the Pre-Raphaelite artist and writer William Morris—and applying it to the modern condition, Nightingale presents timeless messages on crucial topics including, but by no means limited to, the importance of personal development, the nature of and path to success, the ills of materialism, the need to value simplicity over chaos and quality over quantity, the critical role played by the imagination, the threat of environmental deterioration, and the connection between self-actualization and one's ability to enjoy life.

Take, for instance, his incredibly relevant criticism of confirmation bias: "If our ideas come to us only from those by whom we're regularly surrounded—those who live much as we do—we tend to do little more than reiterate and fortify the ideas by which we already live." Decades before social media echo chambers began encouraging narrowmindedness, Nightingale decried the tendency of modern individuals to reinforce their own beliefs and biases rather than open their minds to new perspectives. Moreover, years before bestselling books like *Simplicity Parenting* were cautioning parents about the negative emotional effects of overstimulating toys and frenzied activity schedules, he was imploring parents to embrace the creative potential of what Bertrand Russell calls "fruitful monotony."[1] In these ways and many others, Nightingale went against the grain to champion a mindful, respectful, and balanced existence in which learning, discovery, and creation take primacy over material gain.

In his broadcasts, Nightingale distinguishes between three main "departments of living": (1) our family lives; (2) the way we spend our days, which includes our work and our leisure time; and (3) our income. According to him, "The purpose of [*Direct Line*] is to help us find more meaning, more real success in each of these three vital departments." As you read these messages, you will receive insight about human nature—namely, its proclivity for taking the path of least resistance and its simultaneous need to be "unsettled," to be on a journey toward something that is bigger than the individual—that will enable you to enrich all three areas of your life. You'll surely emerge from reading this book awakened to the great potentiality of human beings that can be missed in today's hectic and overly programmed world.

A brief note on the text: The pieces contained in this volume have been chosen, edited for clarity, and oftentimes condensed or combined in the hopes of presenting Nightingale's ideas in the most readable format possible. As he admits in his introduction to *Direct Line*, he was not necessarily concerned with neatly packaging ideas because of how the medium of radio encouraged mental wandering. He explains: "when you hear something in *Direct Line* that sparks an idea, you'll tune me out for whatever time you devote to the idea. You'll do this repeatedly...because of the way we listen and because our attention will dart from what we're hearing to what we're thinking about." While the print medium still allows for thoughtful reflection, its nature enables readers to pause, bookmark their spot, and recommence their reading without needing down time built into the program for contemplation. As such, messages have been edited to best suit the print format. Another characteristic of radio is that it does not allow for bibliographic citations. When citations for quoted material could be located, they have been provided in endnotes for the personal reference of readers so that they can consult the primary texts that informed Nightingale's broadcasts. A lifelong learner and advocate for continuing education, Nightingale was incredibly well read, and readers will surely want to explore firsthand many of the books and articles from which he quotes.

There is no correct way to read these messages: read them chronologically, topically, or piecemeal—but certainly more than once—and you will receive the same fresh inspiration for becoming a more self-actualized, successful individual. Enjoy the journey toward self-discovery and personal growth that awaits you!

Chapter 1

HAPPINESS

O ur most distinguished and eloquent researchers in the field of psychology and psychiatry tell us that our affluent society has not brought us happiness and joy. On the contrary, people in the highly developed nations of the world seem to be suffering from a malaise made up of boredom, apathy, and general depression. And we know that people are at their best—that is, they are the happiest and the most energetic—when they're striving toward the fulfillment of what seems to them to be good and worthy ideas.

Wherever you find boredom, you'll find the absence of a good idea. People are depressed and bored when they know deep down in the very fibers of their being that the life they're living is not what it could be, not what it ought to be. We suffer from a pervasive feeling of guilt when we're living below our true capacities—in our work and in our play. And it's beginning to dawn on people everywhere that we've been chasing a mistaken concept of what success is all about.

On the other hand, when we're gripped by a good idea—or a succession of good ideas, really, because one leads to another—we're at our best, our happiest; our lives are characterized by a feeling of worth and purpose. Ideas bring the fresh, clean air of renewal into our lives. The real fun of life is in continually bridging the gap that lies between where we are and where we want to be and from what we are to what we wish to become.

There are three main departments of living with which we should concern ourselves and in which we should succeed: (1) our family lives; (2) the way we spend our days, on the job and off; and (3) our income. We'll find success, each of us in his or her own way, when we find ourselves. And when we do, all the things that we want or need will be added to our lives. The journey of self-discovery, the journey into meaning, is the most exciting one on earth—and the most rewarding.

Chapter 2

CHARACTER

The *Oxford English Dictionary* records the earliest definition of character as "a distinctive mark impressed, engraved, or otherwise formed; a brand, stamp."[2] Any person who has had the chance to live as an adult for any appreciable length of time begins to collect about him what we call his "fortunes." They represent a merciless mirror of him as a person. They reflect his nature and constitute in total a distinctive mark, a brand, a stamp.

Emerson perhaps put it best when he wrote, "Nature magically suits the man to his fortunes by making these the fruit of his character."[3] We might experience some difficulty in finding out what we're really like by trying to look inward, but we have only to look about us at our fortunes, for they are the fruit of our character. As Dr. Abraham Maslow, former president of the American Psychological Association, said, "You judge a person the same way you judge an apple tree—by his fruit, by what he produces." Just as you can tell the name of a fruit tree by examining its fruit, you can tell a great deal about a person in the same way. Our circumstances reflect our true beliefs.

You see, our fortunes are simply the sum total of what we want and believe we are qualified to receive at any given stage of our lives. Our fortunes should change. They should not just accumulate as we get older; they should change in quality. If they do not change, it is an indication that we are not changing. If they do not increase in quality, it's an indication that we are not growing and maturing as people. Someone once said to Dr. Robert Hutchins when he was the chancellor of the University of Chicago, with regard to adult education, that "you can't teach old dogs new tricks." Dr. Hutchins replied, "Human beings are not dogs and education is not a bag of tricks."

We can grow through knowledge with good ideas, and as we grow our world will change to reflect our growth. We might say that a person or an organization will grow in proportion to two main conditions. The first concerns his degree of receptivity. Are his windows open to receive the fresh breeze of renewal in the form of new ideas and creative thinking? Many people you know in organizations are closed systems. They've got their windows closed and locked, believing that they are already the repository of all useful information. The one thing that always typifies a closed system is that it ultimately begins to shrink, and it will eventually die if it stays closed long enough. Any person or persons making up the management of any sort of organization who feel no need for new ideas or who do not challenge their own beliefs from time to time are on the road to stagnation and decay.

The second condition governing a person's or organization's growth is the source or sources of ideas. If our ideas come to us only from those by whom we're regularly surrounded—those who live much as we do—we tend to do little more than reiterate and fortify the ideas by which we already live. That's true for organizations as well.

In fact, a person can be said to be an organization—indeed, a highly complex organization. Like any other sort of organization, his or her overall success will be determined by the quality of management. Just as the success or failure of any business or other organization depends on its management, so the success or failure of a person depends on the way he or she manages himself or herself.

We all produce things, words, and attitudes that reflect our management. And the quality of our product—our total product—will be determined by the quality of our own self-management. And the quality of our management will be determined by the quality of our ideas.

As such, we should assess the quality and the importance of the product we're generating in each of our important divisions, what constitute the three main departments of living: family life, business life, and free time.

Let's say a company has three divisions. Two are doing well; one is losing money. The one that's losing money, provided it has been losing money for some time, would seem to indicate that it has poor management, or else it produces a product with insufficient demand. Now, the same can be said to be true of the different departments of our lives. Quite often a person will be great in one department and poor in another—great on the job, perhaps, but poor at home, or great at home and poor on the job.

We control our rewards in each of these departments, for they are commensurate with our management—with our success in interacting with those upon whom our success depends. So, a person standing back and assessing these three departments and understanding that his fortunes are the fruit of his character gets a pretty good look at how he is managing himself.

Chapter 3

GOALS

People have what they thought they wanted. Why aren't they happy? Could it be that they've not moved on to other larger and more worthwhile goals? George Bernard Shaw said that "it is the first duty of every man not to be poor." And I agree with that. Poverty has never brought happiness. We see it staring from the hunger-ravaged faces of the world's underprivileged. We see it in our ghettos. But there are two kinds of income: psychic and tangible.

Psychic income is the income of the mind and the feelings, the kind we get when we look at our loved ones or when we've done a good job. Psychic income is the income the firemen get when they're roaring through the town with the sirens screaming. It's the income a police officer knows when he assumes the authority of his uniform. There's psychic income that comes with a promotion, with the executive suite. It's excitement and satisfaction, and it's perhaps the most important income we receive from our life's work. We can make a living and possibly even get rich doing many things, but psychic riches come from being in the kind of work we like, doing the things we want to do.

In his excellent book *On Aggression*, Konrad Lorenz tells us that the drive to fulfill one's self—to realize, if possible, the potential of one's unique endowment—is coded in our genetic instructions.[4] And it's going contrary to our genetic instructions that causes us to experience anxiety and guilt. We seem to know that there's a way to live that's better than the one for which we're settling.

Family, schools, and society all work to fit us into established "pigeon holes," and for some that's fine. For others, the shoe doesn't fit; it hurts. It rubs and chafes and can become agonizingly painful. There's no psychic income there. So, those people must seek satisfaction off the job in hobbies and avocations or else change their job, because they need to get it somewhere.

As to financial income, it should meet our requirements. What those requirements are depends on individual taste. Our income should be sufficient for us to live in the style we most enjoy, have the things we think are important, do the things we want to do, see the places we want to see, and perhaps help others who didn't manage or couldn't manage to work it out for themselves.

In a society such as ours, not every person can find the kind of gainful employment that forms a perfect fit with his or her aptitudes and preferences. Many factors work to hold a person in a particular place and a particular job other than the amiability of the job itself. But I do believe that almost every thinking, growing, maturing person can find the work he or she enjoys. And for the rest, the deep sources of satisfaction and interest can come from experiences not connected with their work.

Here are some interesting questions for you to try to answer:

(1) If you could completely change places with any other person in the world, would you do it, and who would that person be?

(2) If you could work at any job, would that work be different from the work you're doing now?

(3) If you could live in any part of the country, would you move from where you're now living, and if so, where?

(4) If you could go back to age twelve and live your life from that point over again, would you do it? And what would you do differently?

Studies have indicated that the great majority of people, even though they evince a certain amount of dissatisfaction with their present lives and don't seem to be as happy as they might be, will answer "no" to all four questions.

An attorney friend of mine recently confided in me that although he's accomplished everything he's worked for, he finds himself depressed more and more of the time. He has a fine practice, an excellent income, a beautiful home, and a wife and children to whom he's devoted. In fact, everything is finally just as he planned it for so many years. And for no reason that he can put his finger on, all the fun and enthusiasm have strangely disappeared from his life. He's listless and unhappy, and he can't think of a single reason why.

This has become a common modern malady, and it's what so often happens when a person runs out of goals. This is when the game of life begins to go to pot and the person needs to remind himself of some of the basic rules for successful, enthusiastic living. And the first rule is that a human being must have something worthwhile toward which he's working. Without that, everything else—even the most remarkable achievements and all the trappings of worldly success—tend to turn sour.

Achieving our life goals can be compared to opening our presents on Christmas morning and watching those we love open theirs. We look forward to the day, plan and work toward it, and suddenly it's there. All the presents are opened, and then what? Well, we must then turn our thoughts and attention to others things.

The successful novelist begins planning his next book before he finishes the one on which he's currently working. The scientist always has something new and challenging to turn to when he completes a project. The teacher has a new class coming up. The young family has children to raise and get through school, the new home to buy, the promotion to work for. But for millions who reach their forties and fifties and find they've done all they've set out to do and that there are no new challenges to give them stimulus and direction, there often comes the most trying time of their lives—the search for new meaning. And it must be found if the old interest and vitality are to be restored to their lives, if they're to achieve renewal as people. If they understand this, even the search for new meaning can bring new interest into their lives. They have to say to themselves, "Alright, I've done what I set out to do. Now I must find something new and interesting to do."

The force behind every human action is its goal. What's your goal? Is it clear in your mind?

Chapter 4

PRIORITIES/ BALANCE IN LIFE

We've been taught to live within our means. But what are our means? Do we know what our real means are? As a rule, the man and wife in the so-called average home, on an average street, in an average town haven't the faintest notion that they can sit down at the kitchen table, make a list of everything they want, rank the items in order of importance, and then get everything on that list in ten years—perhaps even five.

How do people increase their income to the point where it more comfortably meets their needs—both their present needs and their needs for the future? A good first step is to realize that other people have everything we want and they will give it to us if we earn it. If our income is not what we want it to be, we must examine our product and our management. We have failed to qualify for it or have lacked the courage and ideas to go after it.

Thoreau said, "If one advances confidently in the direction of his dreams...he will meet with a success unexpected in common hours."[5] The direction of our dreams is often nothing more than our genetic instructions and our subconscious or natural propensities trying to point us down a particular path. The minute we begin to move in the direction that's right for us, things start going our way. So, we need to ask ourselves: "Am I moving in the direction of my dreams? Or am I moving in lockstep with millions of other people because of some conventional idea I picked up from people who don't know any more than I do—maybe less?"

It's also a good idea to reassess our priorities from time to time. The mature person understands what is really important and what isn't. His goals, his needs, are his own. They do not necessarily mirror those of the majority of other people—in fact, they likely don't.

Recent research into the modern plague of cardiovascular disease has turned up convincing evidence that we're bringing heart disease upon ourselves because of our lifestyle—our penchant for speed, our impatience at delay. But where are we going? What's the hurry?

The mature person agrees with the great Swiss psychiatrist Carl Jung, who said, "The supreme goal of man is to fulfil himself as a creative, unique individual according to his own innate potentialities and within the limits of reality."[6] And we can do that without a headlong frenetic charge.

You know, when we study golf under a good instructor, we're amazed to learn that an easy, slow, rhythmical swing gets the best results—in direction as well as distance. This applies to tennis or any other sport. It's balance; it's rhythm. The same can be said about our businesses and our lives: it's living in balance that counts and that gets the best results always. We'll live longer and be in better health, do better, and enjoy it more.

Chapter 5

THINKING

It's only when we're calm and at peace with ourselves that the good ideas tend to come. I think that's why we so often get our best ideas early in the morning or while doing something that's totally routine, such as shaving, showering, driving the car, or walking alone. Most people do not do much creative thinking these days. In fact, they've been put down so many times as youngsters that they've learned to distrust their own ideas. But there's a useful system for creative thinking—one that operates on both the subconscious and conscious levels, drawing on the mysterious stuff of the universe, past and present:

(1) Define the problem.

(2) Begin gathering data with regard to the idea.

(3) Write down possible solutions.

(4) After you've thought about it, talked to yourself about it, and even dreamed about it, then forget it. Let it slip down into your subconscious mind, that great slow cooker that will process your ideas alongside those of the millions who've lived before you.

(5) Wait for your "Eureka" moment, and when it comes, immediately write down the idea on a piece of paper so that it doesn't slip away.

(6) Put the solution to work and stay with it to completion.

We are in the midst of unprecedented, amazing change in the world. My hope for you is that change always represents new opportunities for creative thinking, growth, development, the study of new goals, and the fresh breath of renewal. Although there's still much to be learned, the experts on human conduct seem to agree on two points: one, that the average person functions at a fraction of his true capacity; and two, that the most exciting lifelong adventure is bringing more of our real power to bear on our lives.

Chapter 6

STUDY

Have you ever wondered why the great majority of the people on earth remain so ignorant? Why only a small fraction of the people really succeed at anything in life? Plato gave us the answer in 400 B.C. when he said, "Neither do the ignorant seek after wisdom, for herein is the evil of ignorance, that he who is neither good nor wise is nevertheless satisfied with himself: he has no desire for that of which he feels no want."[7]

The great author José Ortega y Gasset carried Plato's wisdom right into the twentieth century. He points out in his excellent book *Some Lessons in Metaphysics* that even though human knowledge has experienced an almost unbelievable growth during the past one hundred years, most especially during the past fifty, the great majority of people have not only cut themselves off from this growing body of knowledge; they have become, if anything, more ignorant than they were before. And he explains why: the only way a human being can get knowledge is through study. Ortega compares study to paying taxes—it's something that people don't like to do, and something that practically no one does when he doesn't have to.[8]

The vast majority of people will go to school just as long as they have to. During that time, they will learn only what is absolutely necessary, which isn't very much, and they will stop on any subject the moment they're allowed to. That's why we have the mind-boggling phenomenon of a multibillion-dollar school system and a nation of people with barely enough useful information to find the seat of their pants with both hands. Never in the history of man has a nation been offered the opportunities for learning as has the United States and had those opportunities systematically ignored.

Most people sit dull-eyed and slack-jawed in front of their television sets and complain that they're not more successful, or tell a British research team they'd like a 20 percent increase in income. By far, the great majority of them are overpaid as it is. If they devoted a half hour a night to continuing education, they could be the world's smartest people, but they don't realize that. Nor do they seem to know that there's freedom and fun in knowledge.

As I mentioned earlier, if there's one thing that typifies our society, it's boredom, apathy. Whenever you find boredom, you find the absence of a good idea. And whenever you find the absence of a good idea, you find a person who isn't using his equipment anywhere near par.

Chapter 7

TRANSCENDENCE

In the excellent book *The Nature of Man*, there appears the line "Man tends to achieve his being inasmuch as he develops love and reason."[9] Here's where our hope lies—in love and reason; in our opportunity for service, growth, and fulfillment. It's the way to transcend the grubby commonplaceness of existence. The most important step a human being can take is the one that leads to transcendence—even a little transcendence.

Transcendence may be used in a religious or metaphysical context as indicating the existence of a higher power. It may also mean a liberation from egotism and selfishness. Finally, transcendence may mean, especially in existentialist thinking, going beyond one's self in time, reaching out of one's self toward the future. One thing is common to the different meanings of the word—going beyond our self-absorbed ego, freeing ourselves from the prison of egotism, and relating ourselves to reality.

It seems clear that life has meaning if transcendence is achieved, if man does not limit himself to the selfishness and destructiveness of the mirror created by the narcissist. To give of oneself is the only way of being oneself. This paradoxical sentence is only paradoxical in appearance. It can be found in the teachings of the gospels and in the writings of Plato, Aristotle, Kant, Goethe, Marx, and others.

Transcendence is a goal worth working toward, and it is within the reach of anyone. By getting above the dismal, narrow life based strictly on ego and learning to give of ourselves to our work, our families, and our play, thereby becoming more ourselves, we solve three major problems in one fell swoop: how we spend our days, our family, and our income. Our days will be full and richly rewarding. Our family life will take on new meaning. And our income will take care of itself. By really giving of ourselves we will be maximizing our service, which will automatically maximize our rewards.

Transcendence is not an easy thing to achieve, but it is worth working toward, and it can be done in balance, without rush, by getting our priorities straight and organizing our time.

Chapter 8

PHYSICAL FITNESS

Living in balance is important for our physical health and our appearance too. Golfer Gary Wiren suggests that we should all ask ourselves these questions: Are my muscles getting soft and flabby? Do I feel chronically tired? Am I clumsy performing physical tasks that once were relatively easy for me? Can I feel and see unsightly bulges of fat on my body? Do I have to stop and catch my breath after climbing one or two flights of stairs? Is my physical zest for life missing or rapidly failing? If you agreed to more than a couple of these questions, you may well become a victim of premature aging.

We can ward off premature disease by spending just a few minutes a day exercising. I've never been a physical fitness nut, but I believe that we should take care of our bodies just as we should our minds—and to get the best use of both requires exercise.

It's estimated that only 4 to 5 percent of the American adult population exercises regularly. Why? The answer lies in the placement of our priorities. Our scale of values is cockeyed. Think for a moment: What would you trade for good health? Can you think of anything? I can't—because with health we can do anything and enjoy it.

You have to eat sensibly too. One of the hardest things for most of the population to learn is that food intake must match energy output. When we were in our teens and early twenties, we usually had high energy output, and so we formed the habit of eating a lot. Because habits tend to remain constant or increase with time, chances are that a given person will continue to eat the same amount of food, or even more, as he grows older. And as his energy curve begins to go down, the gap between his descending energy curve and his food intake line will be represented by the spread of his waistline and the seat of his pants.

When John D. Rockefeller was in his fifties making a million dollars a week, he was told by his physician that unless he changed his living habits he wouldn't be around much longer to enjoy his rapidly accumulating fortunes. The doctor gave Mr. Rockefeller three simple pieces of advice, and as is often the case, in their simplicity was woven a profound wisdom. This is what Mr. Rockefeller was told: (1) push yourself away from the table while you're still a little bit hungry, (2) stop worrying, and (3) get some regular physical exercise. The health of modern Western man is being destroyed by three things: overeating, excessive worrying, and a sedentary existence.

Let's explore together the possibilities available in our daily lives to increase our physical activity. In my mind, there are four basic ways in which people can find the physical activity their bodies need to function at their best:

1. DAILY WORK

We can get regular physical activity through our work. However, the amount of physical labor required by most jobs today is very minimal. So, in order to offset the loss of physical activity that has beset man in this era, we need to find a suitable substitute for physical work, and that's where the other three ways come in.

2. A PLANNED EXERCISE PROGRAM

The second and most obvious way to increase physical activity is through a planned exercise program. This can include joining a group at the YMCA or your local community center. Or it could be a personal program of regular calisthenics, yoga, jogging, or any number of activities pursued at your local health club or in and around your home. The drawback of this form of exercise is that it can be boring, especially when you're working at it alone.

3. SPORTS AND RECREATION

The most palatable form of exercise is through sports and recreation. Besides the pure fun of what you're doing, there are tremendous rewards that come from activities like swimming, hiking, tennis, handball, cycling, badminton, square dancing, judo, skiing, volleyball, and other activities that are strenuous enough to condition you while you're enjoying the activity.

4. BUILT-INS

"Built-ins" can be the answer for a frantically busy person who has difficulty finding the time to exercise. Anyone can insert these into their daily routines. Sandwich them in regularly and they become a habit. Let me give you some examples. Try holding your stomach in whenever you're waiting for a red light or while you're walking. How about riding an exercise bike while you're watching television? Why not use the time it takes to draw your bathwater for doing sit-ups or push-ups? Sound strange? It really isn't. It's simply using to the best advantage that most precious commodity of all—time.

Now, any one of these four areas mentioned—your work, formal exercise, sports and recreation, and built-ins—could provide you with adequate activity to maintain a high state of physical fitness. But the most successful and lasting activity program will undoubtedly combine all four. It takes some planning and commitment, but you can reach whatever level of activity and fitness you really desire.

Remember, physical fitness is an unusual commodity. You can't buy it, borrow it, or steal it. And once you have it, you can't even store it. To possess it, you must make regular activity a daily habit and physical exertion a part of your life.

Chapter 9

EFFORT AND REWARD

The cumulative effect of a little time well spent every day is almost unbelievable. There are hundreds of excellent courses that can be taken. I think it all comes down to the fact that most human beings form the habit early in life of doing no more than they absolutely have to do. They miss the fun of learning, the fun of achieving beyond the simple chores of their days.

Now, why should we do all this? Why go to all this trouble? Well, let's get back to what Gerald Sykes and other experts have pointed out: the worst guilt of all is the guilt of not having become our true selves.

The pervasive discontent we see on all sides is triggered, more often than not, by the inner knowledge that life ought to be better, more fun, more exciting, and more interesting. And it should be and it can be—when we bring more of ourselves to bear upon it, when we find more of our real talents, when we reach into the deep reservoirs of ability, even genius, that lurk in each of us.

Emerson wrote, "Intellect annuls fate."[10] This means that to the degree that we use the brains with which we were born do we move toward freedom. To the extent that we do not think and learn are we dependent on fate, circumstance, and chance. People's freedom depends on the extent of their thinking, and the extent of their thinking might be said to depend in large measure on how successful they've been in cutting themselves loose from the misinformation with which many of us grew up.

I've long believed that the nagging discontent observable in the lives of so many rests on the fact that they seem to think that there's an easy, effortless way to succeed in life. In seeking what appears to be the easy way out, they actually make life more difficult for themselves. Instead, by following what in the beginning appeared to be the more difficult route—the route to knowledge and self-discovery—and by taking what might appear to the casual onlooker to be a considerable risk, it turns out that in time, they've taken the better and, ultimately, the easier, safer, and more satisfying way.

Sooner or later, we must realize the truth of Gerald Sykes's marvelous statement that "any solid achievement must of necessity take years of humble apprenticeship and lead to estrangement from most of society." Always be suspicious of the so-called quick success. Even towering geniuses usually don't produce their best work until after many years of seasoning and dedicated experience. If it comes easy, it usually doesn't amount to much.

But what about the part about "estrangement from most of society"? To become great in anything is to be a nonconformist and to cut oneself away from the great majority of those in one's own field. The great businessmen, the great professional people, the great educators are all mavericks. The people who wait for innovations and ideas to come from others in their field, which is what 98 percent of people in every field do, can never be better than second best. You can't go along with the crowd and amount to much. The two simply don't go together.

So it's true—any solid achievement must take years of humble apprenticeship and lead to estrangement from most of society.

Chapter 10

KNOWLEDGE, POWER, AND RESPONSIBILITY

In his excellent book *The Age of Discontinuity*, Peter Drucker points out that historically the men of knowledge have not held power, at least not in the West.[11] If they had any role at all at the seats of the mighty, it was that of court jester. There was so little truth historically in the old adage that the pen is mightier than the sword. Knowledge was a solace to the afflicted and a joy to the wealthy, who could afford to pursue it, but it was not power.

Indeed, up until relatively recently, the only position for which knowledge prepared one for was that of servant to the mighty. Until the middle of the nineteenth century, Oxford and Cambridge trained clergymen. The European

University produced civil servants. The business schools in the United States set up less than a century ago have been preparing well-trained clerks rather than entrepreneurs.

But now, says Drucker, knowledge has power. It controls access to opportunity and advancement. Scientists and scholars are no longer merely on tap; they're on top. They must be listened to by the policy makers. And the learned are no longer poor. On the contrary, they're true capitalists in the knowledge society. As Drucker mentions, these intellectuals have a responsibility to society to continue to pursue knowledge for the common good, rather than becoming comfortable in a position and doing no more than one must.

So, an hour a day improving your mind is the best exercise habit you can form and is one that pays big dividends in all three of those important departments of life (our family lives, our daily practices, and our income).

Chapter 11

SELF-ACTUALIZATION

According to Dr. Abraham Maslow, growth toward self-actualization is both natural and necessary. By growth he means the constant development of talents, capacities, creativity, wisdom, and character. Phrased another way, growth is the progressive satisfaction of higher and higher levels of psychological needs. In Maslow's words, "Man demonstrates in his own nature a pressure toward fuller and fuller Being, more and more perfect actualization of his humanness in exactly the same naturalistic, scientific sense that an acorn may be said to be 'pressing toward' being an oak tree."[12] It's easy to see in children, but it's so often lacking in adults.

Psychological growth leads to psychological health. The growth process requires a constant willingness to take chances, to make mistakes, and to break habits. "One can choose," says Maslow, "to go back toward safety or forward toward growth. Growth must be chosen again and again; fear must be overcome again and again."

Maslow also advanced what he called the "Jonah complex"—the tendency in adults to doubt and even fear their own abilities, their own potential to be greater. As he put it: "We fear our highest possibilities (as well as our lowest ones). We're generally afraid to become that which we can glimpse in our most perfect moments, under the most perfect conditions, under conditions of greatest courage."[13] The pleasures of growth and development require effort and self-discipline and a certain amount of pain, but they're worth a thousand times what they cost.

Chapter 12

THE HUMAN MIND'S INFINITE CAPACITY

People who underestimate their ability to think and solve problems should familiarize themselves with recent neurological research. Work at the UCLA Brain Research Institute points to there being enormous abilities latent in everyone. It seems that the ultimate creative capacity of the human brain may be, for all practical purposes, infinite.

Scientists have been amazed by the enormous reserve capacity of the mind. One eminent Russian scholar said, "Men under average conditions of work and life use only a small part of their thinking equipment. If we were able to force our brain to work at only half its capacity, we could, without any difficult whatsoever, learn forty languages, memorize an encyclopedia from cover to cover, and complete the required coursework of dozens of colleges." A statement like that makes us realize how we form the habit of living in low gear—"getting through," as Thomas Henry Huxley once put it, "without too much discredit."[14]

The human brain has four remarkable powers that far exceed anything yet built into a machine. First, it has the power to absorb, to take in information and knowledge of every kind. We do this by reading, listening, touching—by using all five of our senses. Our minds are like unlimited corrals with the gates wide open.

Second, we have the power of retention, the capacity to retain knowledge and recall it. The human mind can capture, store, recall, and program more than six hundred bits of information per second, keeping all of it readily available for recall and use, with unlimited space for additional information.

Third, we have the power of judgment, of logical thought. The more facts we feed our brain, the more it is able to reason and judge intelligently.

Fourth, the greatest power of all is the power of imagination, the ability to think creatively, to take all ideas and combine them into new relationships, to dream, to think of things that do not now exist, to project ourselves into the future with the automatic time machine of our minds. That's the power that's made humans what they are.

As I've mentioned previously, researchers such as Dr. Maslow suggest that people who live close to their true capacity have a pronounced sense of well-being and considerable energy and see themselves as leading purposeful and creative lives. Isn't that what we all want?

Chapter 13

IMAGINATION

Imagination is everything. Our lives will reflect the way we use our imagination. The child imagines himself walking like the adults he sees above him. As soon as he can walk, he wants to run. As we reach successive plateaus in life, we begin to imagine ourselves reaching the next one. And thus our imaginations lead us on from one idea to another through every day and every year of our lives.

But if we're not careful, our imaginations can lead us into mazes of confused complications from which we may find it difficult to extricate ourselves. So it's a good idea, as we use our imagination, always to strive for simplicity.

Remember the three main departments of living: family, how we spend our days (work and leisure), and income. If we're wise, we'll work toward keeping each as uncomplicated as possible—as interesting and rewarding as possible, but at the same time, simple and straightforward.

Are we living the lives we want to live? Or are we living stereo-typical lives that are based on phony values? Usually, they're a combination of both. We think, "Surely other people must have some idea of what constitutes the good life." But when we look closer, we see that they're living "shadow lives," as Lewis Mumford calls them.

In competitive ice skating, you've seen a couple match each other's movements almost perfectly. It's called shadow skating, I believe. They try to match each other's movements so perfectly that they might be each other's shadow.

In any sort of neighborhood, you will find people living much the same way. Their homes, landscaping, furnishing, and lives are typified by an almost total lack of imagination. Most of us make the mistake of not asking why. Why do I live here, in this house, rather than in some other house? Why this life instead of another life? Why this work instead of other work? Why these rewards instead of others?

Now, this doesn't mean we'll change anything necessarily, but at least we'll be living lives that have been examined and found to be to our personal liking. We'll know that we're not living the lives we're living simply because they are pretty much composite copies of the lives we see about us.

We should use our imaginations to make the three departments of living richly satisfying. First, we must ask ourselves, "How are we using our imaginations to bring meaning, charm, and love to our family relationships?" For most of us, the family is the most important part of life. And because the family is first in importance, it represents a fertile field for the imagination. You might institute family creative thinking sessions, in which all members of the family reflect on current behaviors and surroundings and propose new directions and activities in which to engage.

Next, let's think about imagination as it applies to the way we spend our days—our work and our leisure. In the workplace, it's common for people to resist change. But if you have what you believe to be a good idea, if your research causes you to believe it will be a significant benefit, and if the costs and disruption involved are not completely out of line with its ultimate benefits, then fight it through. Do it as diplomatically as you can, make as few enemies as possible, but fight it through if you believe in it. The object of management is not to be loved by the people in the organization; it's to make things happen most profitably for all concerned, particularly the customer. Walt Disney used to ask ten people what they thought of a new idea. If they were unanimous in their rejection of it, he would begin working on it immediately. Our world today consists of thousands of things people once thought were impossible. How many good ideas have you followed through to completion in your work during the past year?

The other component of imagination in our jobs is continual study. We can never get an idea without raw material, which is information and application. Spending time each day building our storehouses of information will produce a never-ending stream of interesting, imaginative ideas that we can apply to our work. It will also confer upon us a very precious thing—freedom, complete independence. We can live where we please, earn the income we desire, and have a wonderful life through the systematic development of our imaginations.

What applies to our work also applies to our leisure—our hobbies, our avocations. If we play golf or tennis, it's much more enjoyable if we play the game well. Again, a systematic, never-ending study of the game or sport will keep our ability and enthusiasm growing over the years.

Imagination is everything in the income department too. Many times, your best ideas will come from other people. Other people can make you rich if you'll listen to them. Time and time again during my business life the ideas of others have proven to be of enormous value. One idea given to me many years ago by an acquaintance earned my company several million dollars. Another idea, a suggestion at lunch by another acquaintance, resulted in my daily radio program. We're often too close to ourselves and tend to take ourselves for granted.

I don't mean that we should follow every suggestion made to us— not by any means. But every once in a while someone can drop a handful of diamonds in our lap. Personal renewal demands that we maintain an open, free-flowing idea system.

So, in our family, in our work and leisure time, and in our income, we should endeavor to use our imagination to help us envision greater horizons for our existence. Employing our imagination to this end will enable us to live more meaningful, and thus more satisfying, lives. As George Bernard Shaw wrote in *Back to Methuselah*, "Imagination is the beginning of creation. You imagine what you desire; you will what you imagine; and at last you create what you will."[15] We can put the power of the imagination to marvelous use, employing it to transform our lives for the better.

Chapter 14

REDUCING FRICTION

I t's important to live in balance, with a minimum of friction. You know, scientists are in agreement that the following biblical admonition is correct: "He that is slow to anger is better than the mighty; and he that ruleth his spirit than he that taketh a city."[16]

If we can catch the vision that life is lived from within, that it's not so much what happens around us or to us as what happens in us that counts, we can set our own pace; live our own lives; meet situations and people objectively, without fear or resistance; and become as healthy, prosperous, and happy as we want to be.

Anyone who knows anything about mechanics knows that friction is the enemy. Steel wheels on rails reduce friction almost to the vanishing point, and an enormous load can be moved great distances with surprisingly little power. We can do the same by reducing the friction in our lives, because the more friction, the slower we must move—and with greater effort.

In all the departments of living, developing calmness and serenity is worth any effort. It typifies the great person, the true professional. The calm person moves ahead. People just naturally look to him for leadership. Calmness also greatly contributes to good health. More often than anyone dares to guess, ill-health comes from emotional stress. Friction is the culprit.

Developing serenity—a calm, peaceful attitude toward others, our work, and our goals—will work wonders in our lives. So, we should calm down and slow down. And with a little discrimination as to what we allow to get through to us, we can do much more and enjoy ourselves much more—with much less friction and effort.

Chapter 15

SINGLENESS OF PURPOSE

When we wake in the morning, there are a thousand distractions poised to get at us as we go throughout the day. They clamor at us in sound and sight; they're frantic, frenetic. They implore, they importune, they threaten, they cajole. If we'd let them, they'd keep us spinning like confused tops. We need to put a sentry at the door to our consciousness and look at the credentials of that which would enter.

We can suffer from inner pollution. We should be choosy about what we let enter our consciousness—as choosy as we are about the furnishings in our homes. A great educator once said something to the effect that the most interesting people are the people with the most interesting pictures in their minds. If you begin to think of the things that clamor for your attention as paintings waiting to hang on your walls, you can become very selective.

I had the good fortune to be raised near a harbor. As a kid, I used to spend hours down on the docks watching the ships loading and unloading. When I got older, some of the mates and skippers even invited me on board. Over the years, I've tried to figure out why I like ships so much, and I believe I've come up with the answer. Ships operate during their lives the way we should and yet often don't. At any given moment, a ship is 100 percent successful. That is, it's either sailing to a predetermined port of call or it's in port getting ready to sail to another one.

A ship owner is smart. He knows a ship can only reach one port of call at a time. You never see any doubt or confusion or him trying to get the ship to do more than one thing at a time. You can climb up to the navigation bridge and ask the captain where he's going and he'll tell you instantly and in one sentence.

How many people do you know who can do the same thing? It seems that most people want so many different things, most of which they're not even really sure of. They're like the guy who jumped on the horse and rode off in all directions at once. What they ought to do is recognize the truth and success of a ship: pick one port that's important, sail to it, and then rest for a little while before sailing to another important port. In this way, in not too many years a man can set and reach his goals one by one, until finally he's got a tremendous pile of accomplishments in which he can take pride. He's got all the things he wants just because he had sense enough to realize he could do well at only one thing at a time.

There's one other point that fits in here, and maybe it's the most important one of all. If a ship tied up to a dock for some reason had no place to go, it would stay there until it fell apart from rest and disuse. Ships don't start their engines until they have someplace to go. And here again it's the same with men.

That's why it's so important that each of us has a port of call we want to reach—a goal, a place to get to—that we feel would be better than the place in which we now find ourselves. If we don't, we might never cast off. We might never know the thrill of sailing a pre-charted course to a place we can't see fully for 99 percent of the journey. But we know it's there, and we know that if we keep sailing toward it, we'll eventually reach it.

Chapter 16

GENIUS

The great William James defined genius as "little more than the faculty of perceiving in an unhabitual way."[17] And the genius, as defined by Dr. James, seems to be that rare bird who knows that change is not only good but inevitable. He habitually looks at everything about him in an original way. He takes nothing for granted. He knows that whatever he sees that is made by man or served by man is imperfect, is always in a state of evolving.

Let me give you a good example. A friend of mine was looking for a site for a large luxury hotel. He was in no hurry and spent months in a certain West Coast city looking for the site that would best guarantee a good return on the considerable amount of money he was going to invest. He found the perfect site. It was near a large university and at the junction of five main roads, one of which was a heavily traveled highway. It was also within the city limits, which would mean a large local trade for the restaurant. There was only one hitch: on the site was an old brick building—an old manufacturing concern still in business.

He called on the owners of the business and told them what he wanted to do. Because the city had grown around the old building over the years, he pointed out that it would be to their benefit to sell him the property at a price many times the land's original value and build themselves a new, more modern plant in a less congested area. The owners saw the sense in his plan and closed the deal. He raised the old building and built his beautiful new hotel.

Later, he discovered that many people in the hotel business had looked upon that site as ideal for their purposes but had written it off because it was already occupied. My friend saw it, not with the old brick manufacturing plant on it, but instead with his beautiful new hotel sitting there. He had looked at that corner of land in an unhabitual way. Everybody benefited from his genius, including the community.

I think all of us can greatly increase the value of our lives by taking to heart Dr. James's definition of genius—by looking at things about us, in our home and particularly in our work, with new eyes, with the eyes of creation. We can form the habit of seeing things not as they are, but as they could be or will be, as our changing world will insist they be in the future.

Our lives are full of old brick buildings that have stood there for too long. We just don't see them anymore. Or if we do, we just assume they'll always be there. And maybe they always will if we don't do something about them.

So, take to heart Dr. James's definition of genius: "Genius...means little more than the faculty of perceiving in an unhabitual way."[18]

Chapter 17

MOTIVATION

"To accomplish anything," as W. MacNeile Dixon writes in *The Human Situation*, "you need an interest, a motive, a center for your thoughts. You need a star to steer by, a course, a creed, an idea, a passionate attachment…. Something must beckon you or nothing is accomplished, something about which you ask no questions. Thought needs a fulcrum for its lever. Effort demands an incentive or an aim."[19] We need to know our motive.

If you'd like to know more about the interesting subject of motivation—what motivates people today and what doesn't—read John Price's *The Enjoyment of Management*. He points out that the five classic forms of motivation have been with us for centuries: pay, direction, discipline, underutilization, and diversion. But do they still work today?

PAY

Pay is income to the person for use as he determines, but he's influenced by a couple of things: Does he have full freedom to use pay in any manner he wants? Or must he use all or part of it to fill obligatory demands such as rent, car payments, the phone bill, and taxes, leaving little discretionary income?

In most people's minds, pay is their due for the work they perform. It does not tend to change a person's behavior from medium to maximum performance. Pay, then, is not a motivator. It motivates membership, and that's all. Money is what the employer uses to attract and retain people. It motivates people to come to or leave an organization, not to perform to the maximum of their ability.

DIRECTION

Denial of aspirations for independence of action through detailed direction will certainly motivate changes in organizational behavior. Unfortunately, the motivation will work in a negative direction, leading to dissension and withdrawal of individual effort.

DISCIPLINE

Discipline, the third classic motivator, still works, but it's much more difficult to apply today because of the changes in lifestyles and the existence of organized labor.

UNDERUTILIZATION

The biggest problem in our industrial society today, without qualification, is the underutilization of people in the workforce. It is in itself a monumental deterrent to maximum individual productivity. But far worse, it has a relationship with just about every aspect of the work situation: pay, discipline, direction, and also the full range of organizational goals, profit, production, morale, and so forth. The major effect of underutilization is turnover, because when talented young people are aware that they're not being fully utilized, they quit. And turnover, as any industrial leader will tell you, is the bane of his existence.

DIVERSION

Finally, diversion—getting people's minds off the unpleasant job is fast becoming passé.

So, it becomes evident that the five classic motivators that have been around since Moses, Julius Caesar, and Cleopatra don't seem to work anymore in today's rapidly changing world.

Price tells us about five more—the stable motivators that do work. They are growth, achievement, responsibility, recognition, and work nature.

GROWTH

Growth is of two types: organizational growth and self-developmental growth. For the person to derive meaning from his job and thus give to that job the full measure of his ability requires that he sense the opportunity for promotion beyond his present position—the opportunity for the advancement of his own personal competence. He will, of course, sense opportunity only if there are in fact recognizable mechanisms for its realization. These mechanisms, quite simply, are discretionary awards, succession planning procedures, merit increase provisions, and personal development programs.

ACHIEVEMENT

According to some experts in human behavior, achievement is the most important of the needs for the organizational member. Unless the person senses that what she's doing is contributing to a greater goal, that she is doing something that counts, she will very likely produce mediocre work.

RESPONSIBILITY

A sense of responsibility is the third of the five motivational needs that must be satisfied for maximum job performance. As a rule, we do not delegate to people the freedom to act as responsible managers of their own jobs. Everybody is a manager if we think of management as involving the coordination of resources. So, creating a feeling of importance and responsibility is the job of the manager today. And unless this feeling is created in the individual, one of the important elements will have been lost.

RECOGNITION

The five most important words in the English language are "I am proud of you." The next four are "What is your opinion?" The next three: "If you please." And the next two: "Thank you." These are all simple phrases, and they're pretty inexpensive ways of recognizing individual performance with personal concern.

WORK NATURE

The last ingredient in the high performance recipe is work content, the nature of the job itself. Unless people have a basic liking for the functions, tasks, and mechanics of the work they perform, they cannot by any stretch of the imagination be motivated to perform at their highest achievement level. I don't mean to imply that people who don't enjoy their work like a hobby are lost motivationally speaking, but they must be in agreement with themselves, if only subconsciously, about the fundamental desirability of what they're doing. No one can induce this last element. It must be there.

There you have it—the five stable motivators that will continue to inspire quality performance: growth, achievement, responsibility, recognition, and work nature. Managers interested in the health of their organizations will work to ensure the motivational elements that can be controlled are present in their companies.

Chapter 18

SERENDIPITY

What makes following our ideas so interesting are the unexpected paths and byways and windfalls that occur along the way—the serendipitous events that unfailingly come to the person in pursuit of the goal. Serendipity means the faculty of making happy and unexpected discoveries by accident. The word was coined by the British author Horace Walpole, who based it on the title of an old fairy tale, "The Three Princes of Serendip." The princes in the story were always making interesting discoveries while on a quest for something else.

The secret of making serendipitous discoveries is to make certain we're following a star, a creed, or an idea. Just as ideas and imagination are the fountain of youth, being on a personal quest absolutely guarantees that unexpected good fortune will come our way from time to time. Whenever you hear of someone being lucky, a little investigation will show that the person is a busy, positive kind looking for new and interesting ways of doing things. As I once read somewhere, good luck is what happens when preparedness meets opportunity.

People who try to play it safe seldom learn about serendipity. Sticking your neck out is the way to woo serendipity. Lurking somewhere within every line of work there is tremendous opportunity. And if we'd only find a star to steer by, a goal worth working toward, we'd see more of it.

The people who find a meaning—a deeper purpose—in their work find themselves deluged by good fortune. A good question to ask yourself from time to time is "What is the star by which I steer my life?" It may change as we mature and sort out the important from the unimportant, but a person without a goal is like a ship without a rudder.

Serendipity—we can put it to work in our lives whenever we wish. All we need is a quest, an odyssey.

Chapter 19

LANGUAGE AND IMAGINATION

I n *The Educated Imagination*, Northrop Frye speaks of three uses of language. The first has to do with simple awareness of the facts of life, and it's mostly made up of nouns and adjectives. This language provides an inventory of what's out there. It's concern is with what is. Then there's the practical language of what one must do to get along in the world, how to relate to the environment, and in its most developed form this is the language of science. Finally, there's the language of what might be, the language of what we imagine could be, the language of hope. It's the language by which we formulate worthy goals and ideals. It's the universal language that speaks to all of us during those moments when we reach unusual peaks of human aspiration and genius. As Frye puts it, "That language is not English or Russian or Chinese or any common ancestor, if there was one. It is the language of human nature, the language that makes both Shakespeare and Pushkin authentic poets, that gives a social vision to both Lincoln and Gandhi. It never speaks unless we take the time to listen in leisure, and it speaks only in a voice too quiet for panic to hear."[20]

Now, all forms of language use the power of imagination, but only the third includes the major works of the imagination. In the other uses of language, imagination functions more as a practical tool, not the designing architect of the creative intelligence.

Frye's book is concerned with the importance of having an educated imagination. According to him, by an imagination schooled through constant practice, the reach of the mind is extended beyond all ordinary limits.

There's something in all of us that wants to drift toward a mob mentality, where we can all say the same thing without having to think about it because everybody is all alike except people whom we hate or persecute. Every time we use words, we're either fighting against this tendency or giving in to it. When we fight against it, we're taking the side of genuine and permanent civilization. The power of the imagination is the means by which resistance to this retrograde tendency is strengthened.

We should listen to that voice that speaks "too quiet for panic to hear."[21] Chances are that what the voice is trying to tell us to do is also best for everyone concerned. So then, through the systematic exercise of our imaginations, let's think about what's right for us and what will bring us the joy and fulfillment that we seek. Gradually, through a little daily exercise, the reach of our minds can be extended beyond all ordinary limits. We'll be able to see through the obvious to the truth beyond—the truth for us.

Chapter 20

INTUITION

There's much that we do not understand. Let's open our minds to the undeniable fact that humans are just taking their first shaky, tentative steps into knowledge. And now I want you to understand that there is a mysterious stuff in which we live, as ubiquitous as the air itself, that responds to the way we habitually think. Now I don't know what it is—I don't think anyone knows what it is—but it's there, and it works. It's a magic kind of stuff that creates out of itself that which we demand, whether we know we're demanding it or not.

A man named Clifford Eckels had dreamed for years of going into business for himself. All his life he'd worked as a clerk in a grocery store for a small salary. One day he ran across a quotation by Emerson that just about knocked him over: "Do the thing, and you shall have the power: but they who do not the thing have not the power."[22]

Well, he mortgaged everything he had, arranged for some credit from the necessary suppliers, and a few years later was doing a million dollars a year in business. He later said, "As I started to 'do the thing'—the things I'd been thinking and dreaming about—I began to discover that I had hidden talents and abilities I'd never suspected. Ideas came to me that I was able to turn into more successful business. In short, when I had enough faith to start to do the thing, I did find that I had the power. I'd had it all along and hadn't realized it."

Most people never learn how to play this game of life. If we were really aware of our own powers, we'd live in a continual state of awe. In his book *The Twelve Hats of a Company President*, Willard F. Rockwell Jr., the dynamic and brilliant CEO of the North American Rockwell Corporation, writes:

> The best soothsayer in the world is still guessing. Face it and train yourself to guess. After you collect all the facts, analyze them rationally, but don't be afraid to add the slightly mysterious ingredient of intuition.... When something tells you that an event is going to work out in a certain way, try to figure out what it is that makes you feel that way. Let your intuition take over at times. It may be highly creative, whether you entirely understand the process or not.[23]

To win at chess or golf or tennis or life, you have to make moves, you have to go on the offensive, you have to take chances. There's no way on earth to figure out the result of every move in advance, and you're not going to win them all; there's just no way. You've got to lose a little too. It's the people who won't take the chance of losing who rule out the chance of winning.

The wise person knows about this mysterious stuff I mentioned earlier—this stuff that over the long run will give him what he's made up his mind to get. And he knows that sometimes this stuff moves in strange and mysterious ways. He's going to get a hunch to move this way or that way occasionally without knowing why—call it intuition, a hunch, whatever. And if he's wise, he'll make a move. He does his best to collect what answers he can up front, but he knows that he can't get them all. Life just doesn't reveal the back of the book. We must take our stand and then wait to be rewarded or knocked down, whichever the case may be.

Chapter 21

SUCCESS IN BUSINESS

For those who strive to be at the top, it's important to remember that it can be reached just as satisfactorily within a large organization as it can in a business of one's own, often even more so. The chances of a person building anything approaching the size of some of our larger corporations during his own lifetime or pulling down the kind of income he can earn in a large organization are not always very good. It's unlikely that Mr. Wilson could have built another General Motors by himself during his own working lifetime.[24] Nor is it likely that he would have amassed the millions he did or earned $600,000 a year as an entrepreneur. He did it all as the employee of a large company. Moreover, with the resources that a large company can command, projects can be embarked upon and satisfactions derived that would be difficult or impossible in the smaller organization.

The key to success in business, as evidenced by a Harvard Business School study, is to not just be a problem solver but a problem finder. Problem identifiers are people who are conscious of problems, who isolate them, and who cast about for a solution—who train their imagination. In a study made many years ago by Notre Dame, it was discovered that while executives were usually worth their higher salaries in that they had the ability to solve problems and emerge victorious from crises, they seldom or never thought creatively between crises. They are like the airline pilot who in thirty seconds will earn his salary for a year by overcoming with skill and courage a hairy problem that suddenly arises, but who much of the rest of the time is content just to sit back and drive. They represent the backbone of their industries, but they seldom form the habit of isolating problems that need solving before they develop. Those who will truly set themselves apart in business are the problem identifiers, the people who seek to identify and creatively address issues and/or needs before they arise.

Chapter 22

MENTAL STRESS

There have been a number of studies that have shown that a person who experiences a cluster of life crises runs a 75 percent or higher risk of becoming sick in the next year or two. The more serious the crises, the more serious will be the illness, unless the person can let crises run off his back like water on a duck. It's not easy, and no matter how phlegmatic we become there are going to be some life crises that will affect us deeply.

Oftentimes people won't connect the effect (the illness or physical reaction) with the cause (the crisis) because of the time lag. It sometimes takes the body a long time to complete its physiological reaction to mental or emotional problems.

We should remember that undergoing a serious mental stress could bring illness or accident unless we're able to shake it off quickly. Daily practice in keeping calm and collected is an excellent method of maintaining good mental and physical health. It will also result in many other benefits on the job and at home. Try the deep breath method. It's a good relaxant.

Chapter 23

PERSUASION AND SELLING

Now here's a good idea when you want to convince another person to follow your line of reason, especially when you're trying to sell something: it's called the "feel, felt, found system" of converting another to your way of thinking. Whenever the person throws up an objection to the point you're trying to make, say, "I know how you feel. Others have felt the same way, until they found..." and here you replace an objection with a positive benefit.

"I know how you feel"—now here you're empathizing with the other person. "Others have felt the same way"—here you're not only agreeing with him but bolstering his point, and thus increasing his security, by saying that others have felt the same way. "Until they found that..."—here you show them the error of their ways, how what they feared or disliked was actually a benefit in disguise.

Feel, felt, found—a way to get rid of objections without offending the person with whom you're dealing. It works with spouses and kids as well as coworkers and prospects. I picked that up while listening to a lecture by my good friend Chris Haggerty, who also suggests that if you're in sales—and this is a great one to pass on to your salespeople—you should obtain and use every day three important items: (1) a cassette tape player, (2) a daily calendar of appointments, and (3) a stopwatch. All three will help you become more aware of the structure of time.

After every call, give a verbal summary of it into the cassette tape recorder, including any promises you made, why you think the sale was made or lost, and so forth. This takes only a few minutes and should be done while the sales call is fresh in your mind. The daily calendar is self-explanatory. And the stopwatch will show you exactly how much time you're spending in front of prospects. As you go in to see the person on whom you're calling—not into his office, but as you actually go in to see the prospect—start the stopwatch. Stop it as you come out, and don't start it again until you're in front of another prospect. At the end of the day, you'll have an accurate record of the time you've actually spent practicing your trade or profession. Chances are it'll be less time than you thought, and then you can find ways of increasing it.

Chapter 24

OVERCOMING OBSTACLES

A long-time favorite book of mine is Kenneth Goode's *How to Win What You Want*.[25] In it, Mr. Goode gives a recipe for winning anything that I think you'll find of value.

One: If you work for anybody else, support your leader eagerly and without question until the time comes that you can demonstrate to the advantage of both that you are, in at least one point, smarter than he is.

Two: If you work for yourself, start moving forward in a straight line. Keep moving forward along that line regardless of obstacles. Don't confuse obstacles and objections. That is to say, don't consider that probable obstacles to finishing anything are possible objections to starting it. That difference in viewpoint may be the difference between success and failure.

There are at least three sound reasons for not stopping for anything until it stops you: (1) If the undertaking is never started, all the weary discussion about any obstacles will have been wasted. (2) When the difficulty of doing anything is advanced as an argument against going ahead, a wrong emotional and personal emphasis is likely to arise. (3) Human judgment finds extraordinary difficulty in telling an obstacle from a blessing. Best and worst are so often the same. Viewed in the perspective of results, some disasters become veritable lifesavers, and some apparent lifesavers prove disastrous. Walter Hunt thought himself a magnificent businessman when he got four hundred dollars for an idea that had taken him only three hours to perfect. But he had sold out his patent rights to the safety pin.

On the other hand, "Believe It or Not" Ripley wanted to be a professional baseball pitcher. He had a tryout with the New York Giants, broke his arm, and, incredibly disappointed, slid back into sports cartooning. His first timid "believe it or not" eased into the corner of a sports cartoon—the statement that Charles Lindbergh was the sixty-seventh man to fly across the Atlantic. That elicited thousands of letters. So, instead of shuttling back and forth from ball games, Ripley traveled the world and made more money and had more fun than he would have believed possible before he broke his arm.

Go slow in your acceptance of obstacles. Consider instead the worthwhileness of the goal and how to steer the straight line toward it.

Chapter 25

CREATIVITY

Creative people see things not as they are, but as they could be. They live in that third mode of language—the language of hope, of the future, of the imagination. They are found in every walk of life, not just the arts, advertising, inventing, and so on. Some of them earn their livelihoods through their creativity; others create just for the fun of it. Far more people are genuinely creative than you might suspect.

The great thing about using your mind creatively is that this ability improves with age. It's one of the great compensations for growing older. Every year of experience adds to the fund of possible combinations for newer and better ideas.

The American moral and social philosopher Eric Hoffer pointed out that throughout history, the great creative geniuses and innovators have been quite young and the older people who head various industries today were themselves tremendously creative when they were young and just getting started. And the latter individuals are even more creative today if they haven't let the status quo sneak up on them and harden their channels of creativity.

So, consider today how you might operate with more creative intelligence, using the powers of your imagination to better your life and the lives of others around you.

Chapter 26

TELEVISION

Nicholas Johnson is a former Federal Communications Commission (FCC) commissioner and author of an excellent book, *How to Talk Back to Your Television Set*, as well as an article titled "The Careening of America. Caution: Television Watching May Be Hazardous to Your Mental Health." In the latter piece, he reminds us that the general semantics scholar, Alfred Korzybski, delineates three categories of mental health: sane, insane, and unsane.[26] His point was that most of us, while not insane, are unsane. That is, we're not living up to our potential as human beings. We're not fully functioning. According to those in the human potential movement, even healthy human beings function at perhaps 5 percent of their potential.

Part of the reason that people in today's world aren't living up to their potential as human beings is because of commercial television. As Mr. Johnson says:

> Television tells us, hour after gruesome hour, that the primary measure of an individual's worth is his consumption of products...his measuring up to ideals that are found in packages mass-produced and distributed by corporate America.... Not only do the programs and commercials explicitly preach materialism, conspicuous consumption, status consciousness, sexploitation, and fantasy worlds of quick, shallow solutions, but even the settings and subliminal messages are commercials for the consumption style of life.[27]

The gospel of television, Mr. Johnson suggests, creates anxiety and alienation in the poor and emptiness and neuroses in the affluent. As we're sold the products, we're given the belief that our world as individuals turns on our capacity to consume. We're given a shot of anxiety for free, told to buy more to make it go away, and find the feeling only gets worse.

Apart from the content, the mere act of television watching is a passive activity. When we turn the television on, we turn ourselves off. As Mr. Johnson says, "If it is true that passivity and a sense of powerlessness are among the most dangerous epidemics in our society today, the television set is suspect at the outset regardless of what's programmed on it."[28]

According to the former FCC commissioner, one solution is for television to portray alternate lifestyle choices other than those promoted by advertising agencies. In particular, it should depict the value of performing "life support activities" like growing one's own food, sewing one's own clothes, etc., which contribute to a sense of personal fulfillment—not trying to do everything for yourself, but choosing one or two activities that appeal to you and make the most practical sense for you. Any way to simplify your life—to make it less bound by possessions and to give yourself a greater opportunity to participate in your own life—is beneficial. The tendency is always to join the mob, but it's not the way to life, maturity, and fulfillment.

Another remedy for the sort of mindless consumption inspired by television programming is the reading of philosophy. Philosophy can shock us into seeing that there are alternatives to our routine ways of reacting to our experience. By sharpening our view of what it is that we do in relation to other human beings, we can achieve a liberation from half-consciousness—a freshened, more zestful appreciation of the singularity of things. Isn't that what we're looking for? Isn't that what will drive the boredom and depression from our lives?

Chapter 27

PERSONAL DEVELOPMENT

The awakening of the potentialities of human beings is one of the most important things in life. As John Ruskin said, the test of a social system is not what wealth it is producing, but what kind of men—what kind of human experience—it is producing.

The gross mistakes of our society—the pollution; the wars; the indifference to the young, the old, the sick, the maladjusted—are obvious and much written about, but the core ill lies in what man thinks of man. We do not need to manipulate other human beings into better conditions. The elements of human improvement are already within each one of us. What is simply needed is an environment that invites self-development.

According to Socrates, the true man is the soul, and the soul has its own knowledge and possibilities, needing from others only help in awakening it to action. Indeed, for Plato, "care of the soul" implies an ethical responsibility to other human beings—a need to help them along the path to self-development. We should thus attend more to the cultivation of our souls and the creation of an environment that enables personal development.

Businesses, in particular, should provide their employees with material that is calculated to help them grow and mature as persons. Company executives will say that the development of these people as persons is their own problem and responsibility, and while that is the case, leaving people to obtain the kind of information they need on their own is to make certain that 95 percent of them will do nothing about it.

Now, what the business community overlooks is that people are eager for growth, and as they grow and mature as people it will be reflected in everything they do—on the job and off. Few top corporate executives have any idea as to the almost unbelievable latent potential for growth that exists within the people they're now paying. The fact is that most people, including these top corporate executives, are operating at about 5 to 10 percent of their true capacity. The answer, in my opinion, is a steady stream of interesting educational material aimed at motivating people to extend their mental horizons and to see themselves as original, enormously creative, and competent people with deep, largely unplumbed reservoirs of ability—even genius—that they probably have habitually failed to use for the simple reason that to get by in society, one doesn't have to.

Chapter 28

GETTING MORE OUT OF LIFE

The other day at lunch I was seated next to a large table of about twelve men. Listening to their animated and cheerful conversation, I learned that they were insurance salesmen, all from the same agency. One said something to the effect that there should be some kind of guaranteed income for insurance salesmen, and another piped up and declared, "Yeah, and it ought to be $35,000 a year." At this, there was a great chorus of yells: "Yeah! Hurrah! I'll drink to that!" They were as delighted as children at the thought of earning $35,000 a year, and other comments I heard indicated that at least some of them were earning more like $9,000 or $10,000 a year.

I wondered, *Why did they choose that particular way of life or settle for what they're getting?* And I thought this about not just the insurance men, but about everybody. What caused you and me to settle for what we're settling for? And if there's a gap between what we have and what we want, what are we doing? What steps are we taking to narrow and close that gap?

If we have a picture in our minds of what we really want, at least the next step on the ladder, it's good to keep in mind that we also have the key to getting it—it's imagination. Any one of those young insurance salesmen can earn $35,000 a year, the sum at which they were whistling and waving their arms. I recently spoke at a meeting of chartered life underwriters in Hartford, Connecticut, at which practically every person in the room was earning $35,000 or more a year. They had found ways of utilizing their personal resources in such ways as to be of more service to their clienteles.

Why do some people not actively seek to get more out of life? It can be both an unconscious and a conscious choice. On the one hand, our culture or early environment can cause us to see ourselves in certain lights, living certain ways, doing certain things, settling for different rungs on the social and economic ladder. We can also consciously choose to settle for less by articulating and deciding on a lower aim. Instead of letting our early environment dictate our plans and instead of selling ourselves short, we should make a conscious decision to actively pursue what we want out of life.

Chapter 29

WHY ARE WE HERE?

Let's think about the question "Why am I here?" We know the physiological reason, of course, but we suspect there's another, more important reason too. Perhaps Dr. Albert Einstein helped us understand more about the laws governing the universe than any man who ever lived, and he believed there was some sort of meaning in the way things are. He said, "The more I study physics, the more I'm drawn toward metaphysics." Indeed, Einstein was much more than a giant in physics; he was a courageous and gentle humanitarian as well, and he answered the question "Why am I here" as well as it has been answered, I believe, when he said, "Man is here for the sake of other men only."

Now I'll buy that. It's the only reason in my mind that makes sense. There may be millions who don't agree and millions more who are unacquainted with that statement, but the truth of it will be reflected in their lives regardless. Even the fun they seek is dependent on it.

If we do not serve others, life becomes meaningless to us. And this, I believe, is behind much of the unrest we find in today's youth. There's something in each of us that tells us that once we've put away the things of childhood, we're here to serve others. And if we remain in positions in which we are not assuming the service that normally should go with adulthood, we become restive, anxious, and depressed.

In a previous chapter, we mentioned Dr. Maslow's comment that people are judged in our society in the same way that fruit trees are judged—by their fruit, by their production (both its quality and quantity), which is another way of saying by how well they serve.

A young person often asks, "Why am I here?" The answer is, "You are here to serve." Your part of the bargain is to so marshal your unique resources as to do the best possible job of serving others. And you will always serve best doing that which you most enjoy, that which best fits your unique talents and abilities.

The next question usually goes, "Well, that's all fine, but what do I get out of it?" And the answer to that of course is, "Your rewards all the years of your life will match the extent and quality of your service." Now, if you happen to want a $3,000 a week income or enjoy flying your own jet and driving expensive cars, you've got to serve in an uncommon way. How you do it is for you to figure out, and this is the challenge that can make life so interesting and yet so exasperating.

But forgetting for the moment what we may want, the important thing is to discover how we can best serve. It answers the question "Why am I here?" I am here to serve others. Now I know why I get up in the morning and what I should spend a good portion of my day doing—maximizing, if I can, my service to those whom I have chosen to serve. How can I do a better job of serving today than I did yesterday? This year than last? As long as I can keep answering these questions, I will continue to grow and mature as a person and I'll never grow old in mind or spirit.

But how do we relate the idea of service to others with our personal goals? We need to find the kind of work that so fits the kind of person we are that we can lose ourselves in it and find endless enthusiasm. When we do, our daily efforts become one with our goals. We then serve automatically. Service becomes a natural by-product of our daily thinking, creativity, and actions.

We are all looking for what is good and beautiful, and we'll be on the road to it when we find that which is good and beautiful within ourselves. There's something within each of us telling—or trying to tell—us the way to find it, and it will, I believe, invariably lead to service.

Chapter 30

IDLENESS

When we think of service, we tend to think of being busy. But that's only part of the story. Idleness is important too—the kind of leisure we need in order to listen to that inner voice, to let our imaginations really take off.

In his book *The Conquest of Happiness*, Bertrand Russell blames modern parents for failing to recognize the advantages to their youngsters of what he calls "fruitful monotony."[29] He wrote, "A generation that cannot endure boredom will be a generation of little men, of men unduly divorced from the slow processes of nature, of men in whom every vital impulse slowly withers, as though they were cut flowers in a vase."[30]

Today's great concern is for organized, supervised, and directed activity. Each year fewer children are being left alone long enough to discover and enjoy the world—the time of fruitful monotony. Too many of us feel we have to pacify and occupy our kids with toys and more toys, games, and television. Television takes up some of the time that would otherwise be spent in creative activity.

Robert W. Wells, a feature writer for the *Milwaukee Journal*, wrote an article many years ago that I clipped and saved. In it, he said, "Children have an inalienable birthright—the leisurely pressure-free hours when a child is thrown on his own resources and forced to become acquainted with himself." Wells told of a time when he was a boy that he found himself terrifically bored. He complained to his grandmother about having nothing to do. He explained, "She took me by the hand and led me out onto the big front porch, where a succession of fiercely preoccupied bumblebees plunged headlong into blue morning glory blossoms. The sounds and smells of summer were in the air." And his grandmother said, "Nothing to do? The world is there. Go use it."

Boredom is a great time for reflection, for using the imagination. I suppose Isaac Newton was bored when he saw the apple drop from the tree and began to wonder about gravity. You can get your best ideas when you have nothing to do but think. Fruitful monotony—don't fight it; use it creatively.

Chapter 31

THE IMPORTANCE OF DREAMS

There's some pretty good evidence available indicating that we're smarter asleep than we are awake. It's a good idea to form the habit of remembering our dreams when we can. As Dr. Erich Fromm writes, "We are not only less reasonable and less decent in our dreams... we are also more intelligent, wiser, and capable of better judgment when we are asleep than when we are awake."

Arthur Goldsmith reports a case in which the owner of a thriving business in New York City took on a partner. Shortly after he made the decision, he dreamed that his partner embezzled several thousand dollars from him. A year later, the dream came true. The partner actually had filched a large sum of money from the firm. Dr. Fromm explains it as an example of how the unconscious mind can sometimes judge character more shrewdly than the conscious mind can.

According to Dr. Fromm, the waking mind is often distracted by a kind of psychological noise or static—fear, vanity, prejudice, overconcentration on one aspect of the situation, etc.—and these emotions and prejudices sometimes interfere with clear observation and accurate judgment. But during sleep the static is shut off, and we can form clearer, more honest opinions, thus more accurately predicting the course of future events. As another analyst put it, "We know more than we think we know."

Perhaps the best answer to the question "Do dreams predict the future?" is a cautious, limited kind of "yes." Dreams express our wishes and feelings. Wishes and feelings motivate behavior, and behavior shapes the future.

Chapter 32

EFFECTIVENESS IN MANAGEMENT

In his excellent book *The Effective Executive*, Peter Drucker points out that the effective executive focuses on contribution.[31] He looks up from his work and outward toward his goals. He asks, "What can I contribute that will significantly affect the performance and the results of the institution I serve?" His stress is on responsibility.

The focus on contribution and service is the key to effectiveness in a man's own work (its content, its level, its standards, and its impact), in his relations with others (his supervisors, his associates, and his subordinates), and in his use of the tools of the executives (e.g., meetings or reports). The great majority of executives tend to focus downward. They're occupied with efforts rather than with results. They worry about what the organization and their superiors owe them and should do for them. And above all, they are conscious of the authority they should have. As a result, they render themselves ineffectual.

The head of one of the large management consulting firms always starts an assignment with a new client by spending a few days visiting with senior executives of the organization one by one. After he's chatted with them about the assignment and the organization, its history and its people, he asks (though rarely in these exact words, of course): "And what do you do that justifies your being on the payroll?" He reports that the great majority say something to the effect of, "I have 850 people working under me" or "I'm in charge of the sales force." Only a few say, "It's my job to give our managers the information they need to make the right decisions" or "I'm responsible for finding out what products the customer will want tomorrow."

The man who focuses on efforts and who stresses his downward authority is a subordinate—no matter how exalted his title and rank. But the man who focuses on contribution and who takes responsibility for results, no matter how junior, is in the most literal sense of the phrase "top management." He holds himself accountable for the performance of the whole.

And what applies to the good executive applies also to the good parent or teacher or physician—or any person of great responsibility. People who do not ask themselves, "What can I contribute?" are not only likely to aim too low; they're likely to aim at the wrong things.

Chapter 33

ACHIEVING FINANCIAL SECURITY

Here's a creative thinking problem for you to work on: If you were to lose your present source of income tomorrow, how would you live for the next twelve months? Now, every member of your family should instantly know what to do, where to go, in case of fire. And we should have a good plan to put into action should our income stop for one reason or another.

As evidenced by the Great Depression, Americans can become destitute overnight if deprived of their jobs. As a matter of fact, many people in well-paid positions, even executives from time to time, find themselves jobless. Unable to get new jobs, they suddenly discover to their amazement that they are really poor. And even many of those who never lose their jobs often discover in medical and similar emergencies that they're as helpless as wandering beggars.

Our Social Security and unemployment benefits systems are grossly inadequate, and the investment realities of daily life are such that few Americans have the capacity to provide for their economic future. Ferdinand Lundberg, author of *The Rich and the Super-Rich*, tells us that unearned income from capital is immensely more secure than earned income from labor and that the security of one's sustenance is the true measure of wealth or poverty.[32]

Accordingly, we may distinguish between different types of wealth. Some forms of wealth are productive and growing, such as real estate. Other forms are consumable and wasting, such as automobiles, dishwashers, and refrigerators. Yet it is just such wealth that leads us to call America "rich." Clothing, household appliances, furnishings, an automobile, a small savings account, and so forth are all that most Americans ever amass. Now, certainly this is an inadequate base for an independent existence, particularly when most of this meager collection can disappear after a brief hospital stay or loss of employment. In his excellent book *Squeeze It Till the Eagle Grins*, Scott Burns advocates for the purchase of a house and investment in real estate to best withstand the vagaries of the economy.[33] His points in this regard are compelling. But regardless of whether you agree or disagree with his propositions, if you're interested in becoming independent of economic upturns and downturns you should make a game plan for what you would do if your primary source of income disappeared tomorrow.

If you're not interested in real estate, remember that each year most people spend 90 percent or more of their income on products and services. The country's business firms do the same thing. What can you do to earn enough, out of all those many billions of dollars spent every month, to live the way you and your spouse want to live? Set aside an hour each day to invest in solving your future financial needs.

You know, just learning that more than 90 percent of the people in the country do not achieve real financial independence and security during their lives gives each of us the responsibility to make certain that we are in that small percentage of people who do. As I've quoted George Bernard Shaw in saying, "It is the first duty of every man not to be poor."

Chapter 34

PROBLEM SOLVING

Thinking with a definite purpose is or should be different from random casual thinking. When you're trying to solve a specific problem, the mind and its largely mysterious powers must be disciplined and directed. During the hour or so you set aside for thinking, have your major goal before you, written at the top of the page of a sheet of paper. Then the mind must cease its idleness and go to work coming up with possible solutions to the problem before it.

As you sit there with your goal before you and begin to try to come up with possible ways of reaching it, you'll notice a very sluggish reaction at first on the part of your thinking equipment. Creative people are very familiar with this phenomenon. Like a child resting or at play, the mind resents being called to task and responds sluggishly like oil in subzero weather. When it acts that way, most people usually let it go back to sleep. This encourages the mind to learn, through many years of inactivity, that hard work is not a part of life at all. That's why it's important that you stay with it. Daily effort soon finds us doing with ease what was at first difficult and awkward.

Write down any thoughts the mind passes along. Do not be discouraged no matter how trivial your first efforts are. You're prospecting in exceedingly rich soil, and it may come up with a strike the first time out. Stay alert and examine with great care the ideas produced by your first sessions. Sometimes an idea that appears worthless at first can be turned around or combined with another idea to form a winner.

Just as important as the ideas produced by these first sessions is the function you're performing. Each day as you look at your goal and begin your disciplined thinking you're placing the idea of your goal in your subconscious mind. Like the incredibly rich soil that it is, it accepts the idea as a seed.

Planting the seed once in a single session will probably not plant the seed deep enough or guarantee its germination. The seed must be planted again and again before germination takes place and it begins to grow in the subconscious mind. And while you're trying to pull ideas out of the top of your mind, a far greater wisdom is getting to work below the surface.

These think sessions accomplish two important jobs: (1) they force the mind to form the habit of disciplined thought, enabling it to produce ideas, some of which may be very good; and (2) they plant the seed of your goal deep into your subconscious mind and cause it to germinate and take root. It's the second function that will virtually guarantee your reaching your goal. As someone has well said, "Be choosy what it is you set your heart upon, for if you want it strongly enough you'll get it."

Forcing the mind to think and then come up with answers for a definite period of time every day sets the great subterranean forces to work. And they'll go on working all day while you're doing other things and all night long while you're sleeping. That's how you get the real hidden power of your mind and imagination to work. By setting your goal, you've given your mind a specific job to do, and it can marshal its massive computer-like memory banks and execute countless extrapolations and permutations, trying a million possible pieces to the puzzle you've given it. And at the same time, another action is taking place: you're changing. Subtle shifts in your personality, your attitude, your manner—indeed, your whole being—are underway as you're being readied for the accomplishment of your goal. And as you think about the goal toward which you're working, it moves farther and farther into the realm of possibility. Gradually, what might at first have seemed like a wild daydream begins to make more and more sense; it begins to take on legitimate, concrete form.

And finally, one day when you least expect it, when the mind is at leisure, *the* idea will appear. It will slip into the edge of your consciousness so unobtrusively that, like a sly party crasher, you'll be only vaguely conscious of it. But then with mounting exhilaration you'll see it for what it is—the idea for which you've been looking.

Chapter 35

AVOIDING ARGUMENTS

Here's a wonderful way to avoid an argument: simply ask questions. Instead of immediately jumping in and disagreeing, ask the other person to state his case specifically and to define his terms. People who like to argue and who will do so at the drop of a word on any subject are people who enjoy ruffling the feelings of others. Willis Sloane once wrote an article entitled "Arguments Don't Win Friends" in which he points out that "arguments are useless and largely ridiculous. They're more a matter of temper than temperate conversation and discussion."

Subjects such as politics and religion can almost always provoke an argument. Racial prejudices can bring forth the most ridiculous statements in the form of arguments for or against certain practices. But if you'll apply this rule—to make your opponent be specific about some point you know backward and forward—you may avoid a foolish and endless nobody-wins kind of argument.

I've found that an argument, like a potential highway accident, can generally be spotted from some distance away, and it can be avoided in the same way. Slow down and approach with caution. In conversation, as in your car, the worst danger is speed. It's pretty hard to get seriously hurt going ten miles an hour, and you can avoid a serious argument that could lead to a lot of heartache just by being extremely careful when you come upon a situation that's likely to erupt into a serious argument.

If someone makes a statement that you feel is wrong or ridiculous, you should not remain silent. As you feel the adrenalin pumping into your system, instead of jumping on the other person with both feet, just ask, "Why do you say that?" If you get another absurd generalization, ask, "Would you mind being specific about that?" Ask questions such as "Why? How do you know?" Instead of trying to prove your opponent wrong, make him prove himself right or discredit himself, which he will promptly do if he's skating on thin ice. Put the burden of proof squarely where it belongs—on the shoulders of the person who started the argument. Then you can sit back calmly and enjoy yourself while he gets in over his head, flounders in the swamp for a while, and finally tries to change the subject. And he won't be so quick to start another argument the next time.

Since it takes two to argue, let's make sure we're not one of them. All we need to say is, "Why do you say that?" or "Exactly what do you mean by what you just said? Where is your proof?" Keep the ball and the pressure on the person who is driving recklessly. It works like a charm, and you can come out of the situation looking professional, wise, and level-headed.

Chapter 36

THE SELF-ACTUALIZED PERSON

What would it be like to be a fully mature, fully functioning, self-actualized human being? This is the ideal, busy, happy person with all his or her faculties smoothly functioning in perfect cooperation. Dr. Abraham Maslow studied self-actualized people, and he learned that they possess the following qualities:

(1) They have the ability to see life clearly; to see it as it is, rather than as they wish it to be.

(2) They are less emotional and more objective about their observations.

(3) They're far above average in their ability to judge people correctly and to see through the phony, and this ability extends to art, music, politics, and philosophy.

(4) Usually, their choice of marriage partners is far better than average, though by no means perfect.

(5) They are more accurate in their prediction of future events.

(6) They have a kind of humility and simplicity; the ability to listen carefully to others, to admit they don't know everything and that others can teach them.

(7) Without exception, they are dedicated to some work, task, duty, or vocation that they consider important; and yet, the usual distinction between work and play is blurred for them.

(8) They are undoubtedly creative and aren't afraid of being ridiculed by others for their ideas.

(9) They are spontaneous and less inhibited (and thus more expressive, natural, and simple).

(10) They have courage—the sort of courage that's needed in the lonely moments of creation.

(11) They are hard workers.

(12) They have a low degree of self-conflict, which means they have a fully integrated personality.

(13) They find happiness in helping others, getting selfish pleasure from the pleasures of other people.

(14) They have a healthy respect for themselves based on the knowledge that they are competent and adequate.

(15) They are not afraid or ashamed of themselves or discouraged by their mistakes.

(16) They are highly independent but enjoy people.

(17) They are motivated by a desire for self-actualization or growth.

We would do well to cultivate these qualities in ourselves if we want to live full lives as self-actualized individuals.

Chapter 37

LIVING FULLY

O ur lives are full of things, our pasts full of events that were once the most exciting things—things that buoyed us up to great heights of expectation and filled our lives with fresh interests. Today, these same things no longer suffice to motivate us. We must consciously see to it that we do not run out of wants—that we can still sit down and make out a want list and find ourselves getting that old excitement again for something new to plan and work for. As Dr. Maslow said to his students, "If you deliberately plan to be less than you are capable of being, then I warn you that you'll be deeply unhappy for the rest of your life. You will be evading your own capacities, your own possibilities."[34]

Henry James, the very prolific American novelist and the brother of William James, who is often called the "father of American psychology," wrote in *The Ambassadors*,

"Live all you can. It's a mistake not to. It doesn't so much matter what you do in particular so long as you have had your life. If you haven't had that what *have* you had?"[35] Well, that wouldn't be a bad piece of advice to have framed and placed in a conspicuous place, would it?

But it seems that relatively few people are aware of living, as they take so many important things for granted. They wake up, go about their days, go back to sleep without once having thought, "I am alive, and I'm sensing this day." It is only when life begins to reach its conclusion that people become aware of the importance of living. It's like those people who have to be sick to appreciate good health or deprived of their freedom in order to realize its value.

People who are aware of living and who know how to enjoy living are like sponges—they soak up all that goes on around them. If we don't learn to live now—if we don't learn to appreciate all that is going on around us, all of which we are a part—we'll always be living on the hope that perhaps the future will be better somehow. However, now is the future that we were thinking about last year. And if you don't make it to tomorrow, will you have enjoyed—will you have even been aware of—today?

Robert Jones Burdette said, "There are two days in the week about which and upon which I never worry—two carefree days kept sacredly free from fear and apprehension. Now, one of these days is yesterday, and the other day I do not worry about is tomorrow. It isn't the experience of today that drives men mad. It's the remorse for something that happened yesterday and the dread of what tomorrow may disclose." If people could take this advice to heart and keep those two important days free from fear and apprehension, if they could never be remorseful about yesterday or concerned about tomorrow, they could lift a great load from their mind, enabling them to concentrate on the only time they have, which is right now. They'll be satisfied with what they have and with what they are doing, even as they strive to improve.

This is not to say that we should not set goals for ourselves. I think we should, most definitely. But once we know what our goals are, we can quit worrying and set ourselves to today's task with the calm assurance and expectation that we'll reach the goals we've set in good time.

Chapter 38

PROSPERITY

Ernest Holmes once said, "Prosperity doesn't just happen. It's first a state of mind." It isn't so much the kind of business chosen or the line of work that determines whether we'll be prosperous. It's more a matter, at least in the beginning, of our attitude.

Few other subjects are surrounded by as many myths and as much misinformation as is the subject of how to become prosperous. However, my friend, who is a psychologist, told me that two questions can usually determine whether or not a person is going to make his mark financially:

(1) How much money do you intend to be worth by the time you've reached a certain age?

(2) How much money do you wish you could be worth by the same age?

If the two figures are the same, chances are he'll make it. He'll become prosperous because he has the attitude that says, "I will," not "I hope I will." As someone once said, "Prosperity awaits man's recognition and acceptance of it." Your financial success already exists, but it's waiting for you to see it and accept it as your own.

Just decide on what prosperity means for you and then head out and get busy, starting with where you are. There's likely more opportunity lurking within your present environment than you can imagine. Once you create the proper mental attitude, the ideas you need will be attracted to you. They'll come right out of your own subconscious. Then, if your attitude is still right, you'll act upon your ideas. But it all starts with the right attitude.

Chapter 39

STANDARDS OF EXCELLENCE

Some time ago there was a news story about a Canadian farmer who sold his Stradivarius violin for somewhere in the neighborhood of $60,000. He sold it to the same New York City dealer from whom he had bought it many years before—for more money than he'd originally paid. This is because the violin had appreciated in value over the years.

Antonio Stradivari, the Italian violin maker, lived from 1644 to 1737. That's ninety-three years at a time when the average life expectancy was around thirty. He worked alone, although later in life his sons helped him. No committee advised him, no one made decisions for him, and his tools were primitive, but none of that mattered. He put himself into his work, and all the world's fanciest tools couldn't make up for that.

When he was finished with an instrument—when he was sure that his work measured up to his own personal standards—he signed his name to it. And still today, hundreds of years later, his name is one with which people all over the world are familiar. Ask someone if they've ever heard of Stradivarius violins, and it's quite likely that they have.

Throughout history there have been many people with similar standards of excellence—authors such as William Shakespeare, artists such as Leonardo da Vinci, and craftsmen like furniture maker Thomas Chippendale and silversmith Paul Revere. Everything they did was done well, not because it had to be, but because they wanted it to be. They did it to please themselves, and yet the products of their fertile minds and skillful hands are still collected and admired today.

Now, what is it that causes one person to take pride in what he or she does, while others give little or no thought to the quality of their work? It is a matter of self-respect, where those in the former group derive pleasure from producing quality work.

Respect for quality never changes. And the person performing it gains for himself two precious assets: one, he's built the kind of security that lasts a lifetime, never needing to worry about his income; and two, his work is a source of satisfaction and joy to him.

Chapter 40

THE INEPT MANAGER

There was once a manager who had all the tact and consideration for the feelings of others as a wounded wolverine. To him, there was only one way to do things, and that was his way. As far as he was concerned, all other human beings, and especially those in his charge, were incompetent. The slightest mistake found him frothing at the mouth, cursing, shouting, and running around like a crazy wind-up toy with hypertension. He belonged to the school of thought that embraced the saying "If you want something done right, do it yourself"—which, by the way, has to be the most blatantly conceited, stupidest remark ever uttered because it assumes that no one else on earth can do a particular job as well as you can. Needless to say, the turnover rate in this manager's department was practically 100 percent every year.

Finally, it was suggested to him, by someone in a position of higher authority, that he have a frank evaluation session with his people in the hopes of bringing more peace and productivity into his department. So, he gathered together his people and asked their opinions of him and their suggestions as to how the department could be more efficiently operated.

Well, it was a revelation. The manager learned that he was not held in high esteem by his people, that they only tolerated his thoughtless and dictatorial methods because of the paycheck. But the most revealing and interesting question came from one of the youngest men in the department. He asked, "Where did you learn to manage others?"

This question brought about a deep and prolonged silence. It turned out that the manager had never studied management at all. He had never in his life read a single book on management techniques or how to get along well with other human beings. It seems that he had taken it for granted that management ability came along as standard equipment at birth.

He learned, in fact, that he didn't know the first thing about managing others and that it might be a good idea if he gave a little thought to the subject, which he did. He began to study everything he could find on the subject. He built a fine library of materials on good management and in the process became a very good manager. The turnover rate in his department dropped to normal, people walked around smiling and whistling for a change, and productivity soared.

The moral to this story is that if you're a manager, you should have some frank, no-holds-barred evaluation sessions with your people. Tell them that what they say will have no effect on their jobs, and then listen.

My friend Chris Haggerty recently made a very profound statement: "The goal of most leaders is to cause people to think more of the leader. The goal of the exceptional leader is to cause people to think more of themselves." And that's true whether you're leading a family, a business, an athletic team, or any other group of people. If a person wants to assess his or her leadership qualifications, this is a good place to begin. Human beings will avoid being manipulated, dominated, pushed around, and misunderstood by others at all costs. They don't like, and won't stand for, being a nothing rather than a something—unappreciated, not respected, and not taken seriously. As a rule, they don't like to take orders or to be used, exploited, and controlled. They don't want to feel that they're helpless, compliant, or interchangeable with another person. What human beings are seeking is to be prime movers, to have control over their own destinies, to expect success, to be active rather than passive, to be a person rather than a thing, and to have others acknowledge their capabilities fairly. To succeed as a manager of others, and to get along with people generally—whether in our families, at work, or in society at large—we must avoid any actions that diminish another person's self-esteem. People will willingly follow the direction of another who directs them in such a fashion as to bolster, or at least keep intact, their feelings of self-worth.

Getting along well with other people is still the world's most needed skill. With it, there's no limit to what a person can do.

Chapter 41

QUALITY VS. QUANTITY

I was in San Francisco the other day, and an article in the *San Francisco Chronicle* caught my eye. It was about a woman named Florence Eiseman who had earned a fortune designing and selling clothes for the children of the well-to-do. It said her secret was in the simplicity of the clothes she produced.

In reading that story I was struck by how much we can learn from it. It's a story that has to be told and learned over and over again. First, simplicity of design—design is to follow function. What is the product supposed to do? Secondly, it's important to ensure the quality of materials and workmanship.

How can we apply the Florence Eiseman formula to what we produce? It would perhaps serve us well to take a new look at what we do and ask some important questions, such as the following:

(1) What is my product or service supposed to do? What is its real function?

(2) Is it doing that in the best and most direct way possible?

(3) Is it simple, uncluttered, in good taste, and of the best materials available to me?

(4) Does it meet the needs of my customers and prospects, and will it continue to meet their needs for many years to come?

(5) Is it the very best we can produce to do the job it is intended to do?

(6) Do we have our customers' best interest in first place or have we made them subordinate to profits?

The test of a good or great product is that it tends to remain in style for many years, even centuries. The architecture, statuary, and literature of ancient Greece is still right up to date—as interesting and as valuable today as it was two thousand years ago. A Stradivarius violin; a painting by one of the masters; good crystal, silver, and china—all have appreciated over the years like good real estate. Now, how about what we do? Will it meet the test of greatness or be useless junk in a few short years?

Chapter 42

APATHY

One man asked a friend of his, "How many people work down where you're employed?" And his friend answered, "Oh, about half."

According to Professor E. Louis Swift, except under the stress of a lot of emotion, fear of failure, or heat of competition, most people, including top business executives, rarely make any appreciable effort to improve their daily working methods beyond the minimum necessary to overcome each new crisis. The Chicago Sales Marketing Executives Club performed a study some years back that proved that more than twice as many salesmen are fired for lack of effort than they are for illness, dishonesty, drinking, and gambling combined. And as for the rest of people, an expert on scientific management, Mr. Frederick W. Taylor, discovered that men and women are perfectly content to coast along on methods several times short of their best. Similarly, Dr. William James has said that compared with what we ought to be, we're only half awake. We habitually fail to use powers of various sorts that are available to us.

It's a fact that to get ahead in the world these days an average person needs neither the industry of Edison nor the ambition of Napoleon nor the cunning of Machiavelli. Any man or woman going seriously to work will, as a rule, encounter unbelievably little opposition. In fact, they will find their fellow citizens slowed way down for their benefit. Because most people work half-heartedly, using only a fraction of their potential powers, putting a man or woman with even a little ambition and a serious attitude toward his or her future into this group is like dropping a greyhound into a race of snails. And it's believed that the majority of people do not take a serious attitude toward the future because they fail to decide upon one. Not knowing where they're going, they have no reason to hurry.

Chapter 43

WORRY

It's easier to win than to lose, and it's easier to succeed than to worry about failing. The reason most choose the latter is because it can be done sitting down.

We have more mental infirmities than all other illnesses combined. Dr. Charles H. Mayo once said that half the beds in the hospitals are filled by those people who worry themselves into them. You know, the mind is like an adding machine: before you can solve a problem with it, it must be cleared of all previous problems. Worry jams up the mechanism. It short-circuits the whole operation, impairing the most valuable mechanism on earth.

It's been proven many times that by a simple change in attitude and mental outlook, the same amount of time and energy devoted to worry could be used to solve our problems. Instead of worrying about the bills that have to be paid, shift gears and think creatively about ways of making more money. Instead of constantly stewing and fretting over a problem, we should try to think of ways of solving it.

Creative people look at problems as challenges. They realize that without problems everything would come to a stop. Problems are what keep the human race moving forward. Indeed, problems are responsible for every forward step we've ever taken—collectively or individually. All industry exists solely for the solving of our problems, as does agriculture, education, and government. People go to school to learn to solve their problems or the problems of others. We've all got problems, and that's good. Without them, we'd still be swinging through the trees and living in caves.

And all problems are temporary. As the wise man said, "This too shall pass." So, if you want to have a lot more fun and a lot less worry, try to put your problems in perspective. See yourself as part of the world, and the world as part of the universe, and the universe as part of a great and mysterious living picture. Seen in their true light, most problems shrink to a modest size. Next, choose not to worry about them. Shift your mental gears. Clear your mind of worry and direct it to the solution of the problem at hand. It has a solution. It will be solved. The same kind of problems have been solved a million times before.

Chapter 44

CIRCUMSTANCES AND ENVIRONMENT

Let's return to that wonderful line of Emerson's that I quoted earlier: "Nature magically suits the man to his fortunes, by making these the fruit of his character."[36] You have only to hold an apple in your hand to know it came from an apple tree. It could not have come from any other kind of tree on earth, for we know the tree by its fruit. You can tell a lot about a person by his fortunes because, as Emerson said, they are "the fruit of his character." They are represented by his environment—what he has, what he is, and what he does. But most people don't seem to believe that their fortunes are the reflections of what they are; instead, they believe that they are a reflection of their fortunes. And thus they domesticate themselves to live in an environment and under conditions that they do not like because they feel that there's no escape.

My daughter used to ride in horse shows until she discovered that boys are more interesting than horses. Between horse show events I used to hold and walk her horse for her. He was a magnificent thoroughbred, alive with nervous energy and tremendous power. With one hand I kept his nearly one thousand pounds under control as he slobbered down my sleeve, just as my little girl did when she took him over the jumps. He didn't know his power, nor that he could be free of either of us. He was controlled by our minds, not by our strength.

Like the horse, millions are daily led through their paces by an environment of their own creation, never suspecting that they themselves have fashioned a halter by going along with it—and that its strength lies solely in their thinking it controls them. And because they do not understand this, they are held as prisoners of themselves.

Baruch Spinoza said, "To understand something is to be delivered of it." So then it is not their circumstances that control them. It is their lack of understanding that their fortunes are the fruit of their character.

Chapter 45

ENVIRONMENTAL DETERIORATION

The problem posed by environmental deterioration is not primarily a technological problem. If it were, it would not have arisen in its acutest form in the most technologically advanced societies. It does not stem from scientific incompetence, or from insufficient scientific education, or from a lack of information, or from any shortage of trained manpower or lack of money for research. It stems from the lifestyle of the modern world, which in turn arises from its most basic beliefs—its metaphysics, if you like, or its religion.

The whole of human life, it may be said, is a dialogue between man and his environment, a sequence of questions and responses. We pose questions to the universe by what we do, and the universe, by its response, informs us of whether our actions fit into its laws or not. Small transgressions evoke limited or mild responses. Large transgressions generally elicit threatening and possibly violent reactions. The very universality of the environmental crisis indicates the universality of our transgressions. It is the philosophy or metaphysics of materialism that is being challenged, and the challenge comes not from a few saints and sages but from the environment.

Now, this is not a new situation. At all times, in all societies, in all parts of the world, the saints and sages have warned against materialism and pleaded for a more realistic order of priorities. The languages are different, the symbols are varied, but the essential message has always been the same. In modern terms, it is "Get your priorities right." In Christian terms, it is "Seek ye first the kingdom of God...and all these things"—the material things—"shall be added unto you."[37] They shall be added, we've always been told, here on earth, where we need them, not simply in an afterlife beyond our imagination.

In his article "Modern Pressures in Environment," E. F. Schumacher says that the environment is condemning our priorities. As he writes:

> Today the same message reaches us from the universe itself. It speaks the language of pollution, exhaustion, breakdown, overpopulation, and also terrorism, genocide, drug addiction, and so forth. It is unlikely that the destructive forces which the materialist philosophy has unleashed can be brought under control simply by mobilizing more resources of wealth, education, and research to fight pollution, to preserve wildlife, to discover new sources of energy, and to arrive at more effective agreements on peaceful coexistence.

Everything points to the fact that what is most needed today is a revision of the ends that all our efforts are meant to serve. We need the development of a lifestyle that accords to material things their proper place, which is secondary and not primary.

The so-called logic of production is neither the logical life nor that of society. It is a small and subservient part of both. Its destructive effects cannot be brought under control so that the destructive forces cease to be unleashed. The chance of mitigating the rate of resource depletion or of bringing harmony into the relationship between humans and their environment is non-existent as long as there is no idea anywhere of a lifestyle that treats enough as good and more than enough as being of evil. And herein lies the real challenge, and no amount of technological ingenuity can evade it. The environment, in its own language, is telling us that we are moving along the wrong path, and acceleration in the wrong direction will not put us right.

When people call for moral choices in accordance with new values, it means nothing unless it entails the overcoming of the materialistic lifestyle of the modern world and the reinstatement of some authentic moral teaching. Mr. Schumacher gives us four cardinal virtues to consider—prudence, justice, courage, and temperance—and shows their application to the frenzied pattern of consumption that characterizes modern life. The fact is that the habits of excess and waste have become reflexes in our daily life. And Mr. Schumacher basically says that we must learn thrift, conservation, reverence for the world, love for the earth, and another sort of respect for ourselves—not because supplies are running out all over, which they are, but because it is right to learn these things. And he says that we won't be able to do it without a philosophy that gives us reasons.

Man is in dialogue with nature. And as Huxley once said in comparing life to a game of chess, "To the man who plays well, the highest stakes are paid, with that sort of overflowing generosity with which the strong shows delight in strength. And the one who plays ill is checkmated without haste, but without remorse."[38] Mankind is being checkmated inexorably. His science and technology have not conquered nor tamed nature, as he once thought. He has only been industriously digging his own grave. The planet can only respond to man through its reactions to his actions, and it is saying, "I'm dying. You're killing me." And when man finally succeeds in killing his generous and longsuffering host, he will discover that he has succeeded in killing himself. He has proven to be a brilliant but virulent species. And after he has gone, nature can begin again to clean its nest.

Now, what can you and I do about the materialist philosophy and the state of the world? I think we can start by re-evaluating our priorities and getting them in line with those of the rest of creation. We can get rid of all the junk in our house. We can begin to discriminate as to what we're going to purchase with our money, practicing thrift and refraining from continuing to collect junk. We can develop and talk about a reverence for life, for the earth, and for each other. We can tell our kids, "No, you can't buy that. Play with that mountain of toys you've already collected."

Now, speaking out against materialism in our society is almost a kind of atheism. And it isn't that we're against the technological-industrial structure that we've created; it's just that we want to relegate it to its proper place in the order of things. It shouldn't be in first place—not by a long shot. We want our great business establishment to flourish and wax profitable, but let us make it qualify for our business the hard way—by producing a needed or much-desired product of the very finest quality. Let's take home no more junk. Let's put ourselves and our earth and its creatures and beauty back into their proper places.

Chapter 46

THE NEW PERSON EMERGING IN SOCIETY

In his excellent book *On Becoming a Person*, Dr. Carl Rogers spells out some of the characteristics of the new powerful person who is emerging in our culture today and the different set of values that he both maintains and lives. "I stressed," he writes, "his hatred of phoniness; his opposition to all rigidly structured institutions; his desire for intimacy, closeness, and community; his willingness to live by new and relative moral and ethical standards; his searching quality; his openness to his own and others' feelings; his spontaneity; his activism; and his determination to translate his ideals into reality. I'm talking," he continues, "about a relatively small number of people, but I believe that these people constitute the change agents of the future. When some part of a culture is decayed at the core, a small group with new views, new convictions, and a willingness to live in new ways is a ferment that can't be stopped." Let's take a look at that new person emerging in our culture and see if you and I qualify.

First, let's consider his hatred of phoniness. Our new powerful person sees through façades and tinsel, outmoded and ridiculous customs and beliefs. Free of the tyranny of things and the opinions of others, he and his family—she and her family—live in a kind of solid serenity where true values count, where things like truth, justice, family, and work take on real meaning. It is in the avoidance of phoniness that real freedom may be found, and one can drop off the rat race with a great sigh of relief. There are no inner circles to which these people need apply for membership. They are the centers of their own circles.

This person is opposed to all rigidly structured, closed institutions. By being rigidly structured and closed, such institutions are effectively saying, "We have the answers. We need look no further. This is it." The new powerful person knows that at this early stage of our development, such thinking is infantile. We do not have all the answers about anything. And just as the maturing person is in a stage of growth and becoming, so is a vital institution.

This person has the desire for intimacy, closeness, and community and a willingness to live by new and relative moral and ethical standards. He or she has a searching quality and an openness to his or her own feelings, as well as the feelings of others. This person is spontaneous, unafraid of what others will say about his enthusiasm and ideas and is determined to translate his or her ideas and ideals into reality.

Now, of course these people must constitute a relatively small number of people—a true inner circle, a most important and influential club of human beings on earth. The qualifications for membership are tough. To meet them takes work, thought, and study—a willingness to find oneself and be oneself. But the benefits of membership are great indeed. One of them is freedom. Another is joy.

Chapter 47

THE SEARCH
FOR TRUTH

When children ask their parents what they should be when they grow up, their parents often, and with the very best of intentions, try to steer them toward a particular calling or profession. I remember my parents wanted me to be a lawyer. When children seek advice, here's a pretty good answer: look for the truth.

Look for the truth in everything. Spend your entire life looking for truth, and you will have spent it as nobly as any human being who ever lived. What's more, the calling that's right for you will come along.

Isn't it true that we try to raise our children to begin with certainties in which we ourselves have no deep and abiding faith? And isn't it also true that most people reach adulthood in frustration—in doubt and fear—because those childhood certainties have crumbled and fallen apart? As Francis Bacon said, "If a man will begin with certainties, he shall end in doubts; but if he will be content to begin with doubts, he shall end in certainties."[39] The search for truth, through the exercise of choice, gives our life meaning and purpose and helps us become self-actualized human beings.

Chapter 48

CALMNESS

Back at the turn of the twentieth century, the famous magazine editor, lecturer, and essayist William George Jordan wrote:

> Calmness is the rarest quality in human life. It is the poise of a great nature, in harmony with itself and its ideals. It is the moral atmosphere of a life...self-reliant, and self-controlled. Calmness is singleness of purpose, absolute confidence, and conscious power—ready to be focused in an instant to meet any crisis.... no one lives his life more fully, more intensely, and more consciously than the person who is calm.[40]

If ever there were a quality needed in the crisis-filled world today, it's calmness and the kind of clear thinking that calmness produces—another attribute of that new emerging person discussed above.

Remain calm. Attend to the day's challenges and opportunities with an even-tempered disposition, serenely and confidently approaching each task with the knowledge of and commitment to your course. I wonder how improved our days would be if we would make a point of going over that little message every morning.

Chapter 49

NOISE

The German philosopher Arthur Schopenhauer wrote, "The amount of noise which anyone can bear undisturbed stands in inverse proportion to his mental capacity and may therefore be regarded as a pretty fair measure of it."[41] Noise is a torture to all intellectual people.

The truth of this statement can be observed by watching children grow up. In their first few grades, they shout at each other constantly at the very top of their lungs. As they move up in grades, though, the noise level drops. And teenagers are far quieter than seven- or eight-year-olds, except when it comes to their music.

The more intelligent a person becomes, the more his voice will diminish in volume. The quiet, controlled voice is infinitely more effective when dealing with others—small children included. Shouting or loud talking is almost always a sign of inferiority, real or imagined. It hurts the ears, grates on the nerves, and causes real fatigue. People who tend to raise their voices when they get angry should try to do just the opposite. They would be far more effective and would retain better control of themselves.

It's very difficult to imagine an intelligent, thoughtful, poised person making a lot of noise, shouting or losing control. A person should speak just loudly enough to be heard clearly under all circumstances.

Chapter 50

NEUROSIS

A distinguished American psychotherapist has said that "no one, as far as we know, is born neurotic. We've learned to become neurotic as a result of our up-bringing.... Our early self-concepts depend upon the concepts that others have toward us. If those who are important in the life of a child generally blame him, he will learn to blame himself. If they consistently accept him, he will learn to accept himself. That does not mean that the self-concept a child first learns is absolutely final.... He can later in life change it... [but] this early self-concept...does tend to set the pattern for later attitudes and behavior."

I came across a great line the other day. It was written by Emanuel H. Demby, and it goes: "Self-confidence is like a psychological credit card." To tell youngsters that they are great is to give them the kind of self-image they need to build meaningful lives for themselves. Youngsters will discover their limitations, their blind spots, the areas in which they have little or no aptitude soon enough without our help. Neurosis is like a chain that we put on our children to hinder them in their development and activities.

If you'd like to examine yourself for traces of neurosis, Dr. Albert Ellis, in his book *How to Live with a "Neurotic" at Home and at Work*, gives us a list of popular beliefs—irrational ideas, really—each of which indicates a neurosis.[42] You can check your own beliefs against the list. Remember, each of the following statements is false and suggests a neurosis:

- An adult must be approved of or loved by almost anyone for almost everything he does. What others think of him is most important.

- Depending on others is better than depending on oneself.

- A person should be thoroughly competent, adequate, talented, and intelligent in all possible respects. Incompetence in anything whatsoever is an indication that a person is inadequate or worthless.

- The main goal and purpose in life is achievement/success.

- One should blame oneself severely for all mistakes and wrongdoings. Punishing oneself for errors will help prevent future mistakes.

- A person should blame others for their mistakes and bad behaviors and get upset about the errors and faults of others.

- Because a certain thing once strongly affected one's life, it should affect it indefinitely.

- Because parents or society taught the acceptance of certain traditions, one must go on unthinkingly accepting these traditions.

- If things are not the way one would like them to be, it is a catastrophe.

- Other people should make things easier for us.

- No one should have to put off present pleasures for future gains.

- Avoiding life's difficulties and responsibilities is better than facing them.

- Inertia and inaction are necessary and/or pleasant.

- One should rebel against doing things, regardless of how necessary they are, if doing them is unpleasant.

- Happiness is usually externally caused or created by outside persons or events.

- A person has virtually no control over his or her emotions and cannot help feeling bad on many occasions.

- If something is or may be dangerous or injurious, one should be seriously concerned about it.

- Worrying about a possible danger will help ward it off or decrease its effect.

Well, how did you do?

Getting back to our saying that "self-confidence is a kind of psychological credit card," I don't think enough has been said about the power of positive expectation. It's truly amazing, and there's simply no explaining it, how when we confidently expect something worthwhile to materialize in our lives, it invariably does. It gives each of us a kind of magic wand with which we can bring all sorts of interesting and rewarding events and things into our lives. Those who have cultivated this power, who consciously and actively work at it regularly, do the most amazing things.

We're often taught as youngsters to expect the worst. How many times have we heard someone say, "If you don't expect to succeed, you won't be disappointed"? If you have trouble confidently expecting a successful outcome, a reminder card placed where you'll see it every morning when you get up and at odd times throughout the day can help you get on course and form a very valuable new habit.

Chapter 51

COURAGE

In 1965, Robert N. Mandry, a copyeditor at the *Cleveland Plain Dealer*, sailed from the United States to England in a thirteen-and-a-half-foot sailboat. He traveled 3,200 miles across the North Atlantic in a boat so small you'd hesitate to take it out on Lake Michigan or Long Island Sound. For seventy-eight days, Mandry and his tiny thirty-six-year-old sailboat battled one of the toughest stretches of saltwater on earth. On several occasions, he was knocked overboard by heavy tides, and each time he'd haul himself back on board by a lifeline he kept tied around himself and his boat.

What made him do this? It wasn't publicity. He went about the whole thing so quietly that practically no one knew what he was up to. The reason he did it was that he had dreamed of sailing the Atlantic ever since he'd been a small boy. So, he bought the dinky old boat for $250, completely rebuilt it, taught himself navigation, and practiced long-distance sailing on Lake Erie. He told his wife, "There's a time when one must decide to risk everything to fulfill one's dreams or sit for the rest of one's life in the backyard."

Courage—the courage to take one's life into one's own hands and go after the big dream—has a way of making dreams come true. Robert Louis Stevenson wrote that "courage and intelligence are the two qualities best worth a good man's [or woman's] cultivation."[43] Courage seems to open hidden doorways from which good things begin to point the way. It's never easy, and the good results come only after we've made the journey in our own way. For Mandry at forty-seven years of age, it was sailing three thousand miles of the North Atlantic. Each of us must make our own voyage to fulfillment in our own way or sit in the backyard.

The fear of life is the favorite disease of the twentieth century. Too many people are afraid of tomorrow. Their happiness is poisoned by a phantom. As William Lyon Phelps points out, "We look backward too much and we look forward too much. Thus we miss the passing moment. In our regrets and our apprehensions, we miss the only eternity of which man can be absolutely sure, the eternal Present. For it is always now."[44] Instead of chagrin over the past and anxiety over the future, suppose we consider our opportunity. As Emerson put it, "Write it on your heart that every day is the best day in the year. No man has learned anything rightly until he knows that every day is Doomsday"[45]—"Today is a king in disguise."[46]

Chapter 52

A PRESCRIPTION FOR MENTAL HEALTH

A study performed by two doctors at the Menninger Foundation came up with a prescription for good mental health. According to this study, mentally healthy people behave consistently in five important ways.

One: They have a wide variety of sources of gratification. This does not mean that they move frenetically from one activity to another but that they find pleasure in many different ways and from many different things. If for any reason they lose some of their sources of gratification, they have others to which they can turn.

Two: Mentally healthy people are flexible under stress. This simply means that they can roll with the punches.

When faced with problems, they see alternate solutions. Flexibility under stress is closely related to having a wide variety of sources of gratification. With more supports on which to fall back, a person is less threatened by situations that produce fear and anxiety.

Three: They recognize and accept their limitations and their assets. Put another way, they have a reasonably accurate picture of themselves, and they like what they see. That does not mean that they're complacent or narcissistic but that they know they cannot be anyone else, and that's alright with them.

Four: They treat other people as individuals. People who are preoccupied with themselves pay only superficial attention to others. They're so tied up in themselves that they can't observe the subtleties of another person's feelings, nor can they really listen. Mentally healthy people really care about how other people are feeling.

Five: Mentally healthy people are active and productive. They use their resources on their behalf and on the behalf of others. They do what they do because they like to do it and enjoy using their skills. They do not feel driven to produce to prove themselves. They seek achievement for what they can do, not for what they can be. For when people try to be something or someone, they are never satisfied with themselves, even if they achieve their desired goal.

How many of these qualities do you have? If you're desiring to cultivate more of them, the best way to do so is to embrace life as a process of becoming. Live life to the fullest, pursuing self-actualization, simplicity, and truth, and you will likely enjoy good mental health.

Chapter 53

THE IMPORTANCE
OF READING

The last time I checked the statistics I think they indicated that only about 4 percent of the adults in this country have bought a book within the past year. That's dangerous. It's extremely important that we keep ourselves in the top 5 or 6 percent. Reading good books is not something to indulge in as a luxury; it's a necessity for anyone who intends to give his or her life and work a touch of quality. The truest wealth is not what we put into our piggy banks but what we develop in our heads.

You do not read a book for the book's sake but for your own. You may read because in your high-pressure life, you need periods of relief, and yet you recognize that peace of mind does not mean numbness of mind. You may read because you never had an opportunity to go to college and books give you a chance to get something you missed. You may read because your job is routine and books give you a feeling of depth and life. You may read because you did go to college. You may read because you see social, economic, and philosophical problems that need solutions and you believe that the best thinking of the past ages may be useful in your age too. You may read because you're tired of the shallowness of contemporary life, bored by the current conversational commonplaces, and wearied of shoptalk and gossip about people. Whatever your main personal reason, you will find that reading gives knowledge, creative power, satisfaction, and relaxation. It cultivates your mind by exercising its faculties.

Books are a source of pleasure—the purest and most lasting. They enhance your sensation of the interestingness of life. Reading them is not a violent pleasure, like the gross enjoyment of an uncultivated mind, but a subtle delight. Reading dispels prejudices that hem in our minds to narrow spaces. You can no more be a healthy person mentally without reading substantial books than you can be a vigorous person physically without eating solid food.

I've often been struck by the meager libraries of so-called business executives. I guess they believe that managerial and creative talent and know-how is supposed to come to them in dreams and that they're somehow above the need to read the words of others. They're quite mistaken, and they are, more often than not, holding their jobs only because of a shortage of real management talent today.

I believe you can judge the reaches of a person's mind and capacities, as well as his or her real interests, by examining his or her library. I have known so-called experts on various subjects who don't own ten books on that subject. They just keep saying the same things over and over again, hoping, I suppose, for a fresh audience every time they speak.

There's only one way to obtain knowledge, and that is through study—through reading. But as Ortega said, "Studying is for most people like paying income taxes."[47] They'll never do it unless they have to. A good idea would be to provide a bookcase in every junior office. Then, from time to time, make the rounds and watch the bookcases. Their growing contents, or the lack thereof, will give you an excellent yardstick for determining future promotion—or the lack of it.

Chapter 54

OUR NATURAL ASSIGNMENT

Emerson wrote, "Do that which is assigned you and you cannot hope too much or dare too much."[48] He wasn't talking about what we're assigned to do by other people. He was talking about our natural assignment—that which has been built into our bones and fibers, the unseen nature of our very being. A thousand people may work for a living at the same trade, but each of them has abilities and talents that are uniquely his own. It's through the development and fulfillment of our inborn facility that we can achieve a degree of greatness in our lives. If we never find our strong characteristic, it's because not knowing we had it, we failed to look for it.

Many people, because of their own mistaken idea about security, remain at jobs they don't like and for which they have no real aptitude. Thus they often shackle themselves to a slow shuffle when, had they followed their real stars, they could have known so much more in the way of inner satisfaction and reward. Sometimes well-meaning family and friends can help their loved ones discern their real talent; other times it takes a commitment to self-discovery.

In the Sermon on the Mount, we're told, "Ask, and it shall be given you; seek, and ye shall find; knock, and it shall be opened unto you."[49] Finding our strong point is a good place to put this advice to work. Only in this way can we take the advice of Thoreau and "suck out all the marrow from life."[50]

Chapter 55

FAITH

My old friend, Dr. Harold Blake Walker of Evanston, sent me something some time back that I enjoyed tremendously, and I think you will too. He wrote:

> We live by faith or we do not live at all. Either we venture or we vegetate. If we venture, we do so by faith, simply because we cannot know the end of anything at its beginning. We risk marriage on faith or we stay single. We prepare for a profession by faith or we give up before we start. By faith we move mountains or we're stopped by molehills.
>
> Faith, however, is not often tranquil and steady. It ebbs and flows like the tides of the restless sea.... Yesterday we began the day with confident hope, with trust in its promise. Last night, perhaps after a trying and troublesome day, we

were beset by doubt and anxiety. We grope and fumble in search of certainty, wishing we could escape the doubts that haunt us. The peril is that we shall cease groping on through our doubts and live only on our negations.

What we need, you and I, is faith strong enough to bear the burden of our doubts. No man ever drilled an oil well without being troubled by misgivings as the drill chewed downward toward producing structures, but only a fool would cease drilling halfway to the hoped-for pool.

It was the painter William Morris who wrote, "Into the painting of every picture that is worth anything there comes a period of doubt and despair. The artist, however, goes on with his work beyond his doubt to creative achievement."

Faith enough to carry our doubts—perhaps it's all we can manage when fears assail and doubts annoy. Maybe we can do no more than grope on through our uncertainties, pursuing the enterprises of our lives with the trust that the end will justify the struggle.

If, despite our gnawing doubts, we can muster faith enough to take a single step on the road to where we're going, we are on the way to creative achievement. Every triumph of the human spirit begins with one step taken in faith. The single step is the small handle to great matters. No man or woman ever achieved a worthy triumph without faith to keep going at least five minutes longer.

There's one further thing to be said—namely, that worthy triumphs cannot be won without faith enough to maintain our integrity. One of the ultimate tests of faith is our capacity to go on believing that somehow right is right, even when right is on the scaffold and wrong seems to be on the throne.

All of the great ventures of our lives require faith enough to bear the burden of our doubts so that we're able to take the first step in the direction in which we wish to go—faith enough to keep on going through struggle and strain and to maintain integrity on the way. Yes, "faith is the assurance of things hoped for, the conviction of things not seen."[51] And we need to exchange a life of doubt diversified by faith for a life of faith diversified by doubt.

Chapter 56

SECURITY

The other day I came across the following line by Emerson: "People wish to be settled; only as far as they are unsettled is there any hope for them."[52] That takes some thinking to understand, but it's one of those statements we know intuitively to be true. Even though we strive to become settled and seek the mirage of security, we know that we do our best, think our best, accomplish the most, and most certainly live more fully when we're unsettled.

There's a security of a kind available to each of us—more than we require, really—but it's inside, not outside of us. It is in the development of ourselves as truly productive beings—as loving and thinking persons—that real and lasting security is to be found. If we're not secure as persons, we will only stew and worry about other sorts of security that come from being settled. When human beings become settled, they get nervous and querulous and start snapping at each other. They turn inward upon themselves and become unhappy. They find that the very thing for which they've striven for so long is not what they want at all—that the fun was in the journey.

How often a successful man hears his wife say, "It was a lot more fun when we were living in a walk-up apartment and counting our pennies to make ends meet. We were happiest then." And the fact is that they probably were, but did they know it then?

Living on the edge, striving toward goals, brings out either the very best or the very worst in people. If they're wise, it brings out the best. If they're ignorant, it brings out the worst. But being settled—"having it made," as we say—seldom brings much enthusiasm. Emerson also said, "Nothing great was ever achieved without enthusiasm," and we are most enthusiastic when we are as yet unsettled.[53]

Chapter 57

BUSINESS PHILOSOPHY

Attached to the telephone of a young executive I know is a small sign that reads: "God, give me the wisdom to be as smart as my customers." There's a ton of good sense and a world of opportunity for growth lurking in that small pithy statement.

The primary function of any organization is to help man enjoy a more meaningful existence. If it isn't meeting that qualification, the people in it should get into something else. A day should never pass in which people in business do not ask themselves, "How can we do a better job of serving our customers?"

However, the number of businessmen who ask themselves that question every day could easily fit in the backseat of a

Volkswagen Beetle. Instead of concentrating on a cash register, if they would concentrate more on serving the customer, the cash register would take care of itself. We shouldn't get our causes and effects mixed up. By making our product or service right, everything else will fall into place. It's just a matter of time and perseverance. But we should never underestimate customers' natural desire for quality and value and their concern for time and money. The businesspeople who have kept these considerations at the forefront of their minds have prospered.

"God, give me the wisdom to be as smart as my customers." And we might add: "And to serve them as I enjoy being served when the positions are reversed." The business of thinking in unhabitual ways can also bring a fresh breath of renewal into a business.

Chapter 58

IDEAS

The psychologist Alfred Adler once said, "I am grateful for the idea that has used me." There are millions of great ideas in the world waiting for men and women to use them, waiting for people to dedicate their minds, hearts, spirits, eyes, ears, hands, arms, and legs to putting those ideas into action. Ideas use people when people work for those ideas, when people are dominated by those ideas and make them a part of themselves. The ideas need not be world-shaking; they can be limited and still be meaningful. The idea of a new school in a community, a new church, or another project that will contribute in large or small measure to mankind is incredibly beneficial. Ideas by themselves do nothing, but used by men their effects can be far-reaching.

It's important not only to find something to do but to let yourself be swept up and along by an idea that's bigger than you are. Find an idea that you think is interesting and exciting and jump into it with both feet, head, hands, and heart. Let a great idea use you.

A great idea might be to build and operate the best business of its kind. A business motivated by a great idea will succeed over and above a business operating only for profit. So will a career in anything—sales, law, medicine, farming. A person moved by an idea that's bigger than he is can move a lot of mountains during his lifetime.

The supply of great ideas is inexhaustible. Let a great idea use you. Stand up for it. Work for it. Teach it. Sell it. Crusade for it. Help a great idea become a reality through you.

Chapter 59

DECIDOPHOBIA

One dilemma faced by most human beings in our modern society is the matter of making decisions. We've learned that ours is the only species on earth whose natural state is one of disorientation, and, therefore, all of us must create our own world, even if it consists of nothing more than playing copycat—closing our eyes and ears and blindly following the person in front of us, hoping that somehow he or the person he's following knows where he's going and that when they get there they'll both like it.

We'd like to think that we're intelligent and effective decision-makers. But the facts seem to indicate that we're not and that we use all kinds of dodges to keep from making decisions. According to Princeton philosopher Walter Kaufmann, who wrote a book entitled *Without Guilt and Justice: From Decidophobia to Autonomy*, there are ten major copouts that most of us use to avoid making decisions, and these ten avoidance techniques fall under the larger categories of Type A and Type B drifting.[54] Type A drifters go through the motions every day without giving their routines any additional thought, whereas Type B drifters, also called "foolers," try to give the impression that they're in revolt against the so-called status quo by dropping out of life.

What we're seeking, as Professor Kaufmann points out, is *autonomy*—authenticity as sovereign persons. How does one go about making decisions on his own, decisions calculated to bring him face to face with the best possible life for him? He goes by his gut feelings. He listens to the voice within, knowing that Thoreau was right when he said, "If one advances confidently in the direction of his dreams, and endeavors to life the life which he has imagined, he will meet with a success unexpected in common hours."[55] This means not sitting and wallowing in our old beliefs but moving out of them into new, fresh territory. It means asking the question "Am I living by my standards or by the standards of those about me?"

Achievement is not the most important thing. Authenticity is. The authentic person experiences the reality of himself by knowing himself, being himself, and becoming a credible, responsive person. He actualizes his own unprecedented uniqueness and appreciates the uniqueness of others. This is what makes someone a winner. While everyone has moments of autonomy, if only fleeting, winners are able to sustain their autonomy over ever-increasing periods of time. They may make the wrong decisions sometimes and lose ground occasionally, but in spite of these setbacks they maintain a basic faith in themselves and continue to make decisions accordingly.

Winners are not afraid to do their own thinking and to use their own knowledge. They can separate facts from opinion and don't pretend to have all the answers. They listen to others, evaluating what they say, but they come to their own conclusions. And while they can admire and respect other people, they are not totally defined, demolished, bound, or awed by them. Winners do not act helpless or play the blame game. Instead, they assume responsibility for their own life. They do not give others false authority over them. They are their own boss, and they know it.

They key word in our thinking, in our conduct, in our goals, and in our lives should be *authenticity*. We need to become what we are.

Chapter 60

A THERAPEUTIC SENSE OF HUMOR

In his book *Laughter & Liberation*, psychologist Harvey Mindess points out that everyone seems to realize the importance of a sense of humor.[56] Indeed, the ability to see the funny side of things and to laugh at ourselves and our troubles is an asset of the greatest magnitude. It can help us contend with adversity, derive greater joy out of living, and maintain our sanity. Yet no one seems to know how to cultivate a sense of humor.

The kind of humor that deserves to be called "therapeutic" is not the kind that enjoys jokes and comic routines. For delightful as they may be, they are contrived and superficial, bearing about the same relation to therapeutic humor as pretty pictures do to real art. The kind of sense of humor that can help us maintain our sanity moves beyond jokes, beyond wit, and beyond laughter itself. It must constitute a frame of mind, a point of view, a far-reaching attitude toward life.

A cluster of qualities characterizes this peculiar frame of mind:

(1) *Flexibility*—the willingness to examine every side of every issue (and every side of every side).

(2) *Spontaneity*—the ability to leap from one mood or mode of thought to another.

(3) *Unconventionality*—freedom from the values of a person's place, time, and profession.

(4) *Shrewdness*—the refusal to believe that anyone, least of all himself or herself, is what they seem to be.

(5) *Playfulness*—the perspective that life is a tragic comic game that nobody wins but that does not have to be won to be enjoyed.

(6) *Humility*—that elusive quality whereby a person can shrug off the meaninglessness of his or her profoundest thoughts.

These six qualities constitute the type of humor that everyone needs.

Chapter 61

MATURITY

Do you know what typifies the healthy-minded, mature person perhaps more than anything else? In my opinion, it's the simplicity of his needs. If you'll think back to the truly great men and women of our time, going all the way back in recorded history, you'll find that their lives were characterized by simplicity. Think of Edison, Einstein, Schweitzer, Gandhi, Buddha, Socrates, Epictetus, Christ—all the truly great ones had lives freed from the weight of possessions. Now, they were all people who lived in the spiritual and mental realms and who were not concerned with their own earthly existence, and we cannot be completely like them. But we can simplify our lives until we have them under our control instead of it being the other way around. The question becomes, "Do I own the things I own for my own pleasure and convenience or to impress those about me?" The really mature person couldn't care less whether he or she impresses anyone or not.

If you're interested in making an assessment of your degree of maturity, look at the things that you think are important in life. Mature people carry their important possessions within. They aren't concerned too much about what others might think. Despite the fact that the desire to copy others is deeply ingrained in the human organism, they rise above by not feeling the need to follow trends or fads. Nor do they need to make an impression on anyone. They see life in a clearer, truer light.

It's perfectly natural that the person who lacks inner direction will attempt to find direction in a group of some kind. This is not to say that we should not belong to organizations, only that we should try to find out what is important to us and go our own way—or perhaps I should say "grow our own way." To be great at anything is to be a nonconformist. As Mark Twain said, "Whenever you find yourself on the side of the majority, it is time to reform."[57]

Chapter 62

SUCCESS

Some time ago, the editors of a business magazine conducted a survey on what qualities it takes to be successful. They didn't indicate what they meant by "successful," but because the survey was conceived by the editors of a business magazine it was naturally assumed that what was meant was success in business.

Well, interestingly enough, the same No. 1 quality emerged for success in business that came up for success as a father or mother. Do you know what that single quality is? Integrity.

Children who are taught the importance of integrity never seem to lose it. It becomes a part of their being, their way of doing things, and more than anything else it will guarantee their success in life.

Integrity is what a man wants in his wife and she in him. That's what we look for and hope for in a doctor or a dentist, the man who designs and builds our home, the man for whom we work, and the people who work for us. It's what we want more than anything else in a politician or an appointed official, in a judge and police officers.

Integrity is honesty, but it is much more than the superficial kind of honesty that keeps a person from stealing or cheating. Integrity is a state of mind and character that goes all the way through—like good solid construction.

If a person is offered a large bribe and for an instant weighs the size of the bribe against the chance of discovery, he's not an integrous person. He's simply an expedient person playing it safe, a basic crook. The integrous person cannot countenance a bribe. It goes against his grain.

For most people it would seem that getting through life is a matter of striking a balance between integrity and expediency. Integrity is all well and good, and everybody would like to have the word apply to them, but there are times when people think it's best to wink at integrity and indulge in a little larceny or remain silent when to speak one's mind might result in a loss of popularity or ostracism of some kind. The old battle cry of the mob is, "Everybody does it. Why shouldn't I?" And that's exactly why the person of integrity doesn't do it.

Integrity in business is the surest way on earth to succeed. Sometimes it might seem that what you're doing is going to cut into profits, but it inevitably ends up increasing profits.

I was talking to a well-known, highly respected Florida real estate man the other day, and this subject came up. He's been in the real estate business in Florida for more than thirty years and has long been a champion of going the extra mile. He told me that the more he works for the good of the consumer, the customer, and the community at large, the more money he makes. If he can get by putting five lots on a piece of property and digging the canal five feet deep, he puts three lots on it and digs the canal twelve feet deep. And if the code requires a landfill of five feet, he makes it seven feet. By doing so, he's earned the admiration and respect of everyone in the community, has built a tremendous reputation for integrity, and has become a millionaire in the process. When we make the well-being of people our priority, we'll never make a mistake. People first, profit last—the more you do it, the bigger and better your profits become.

Earlier I quoted Emanuel H. Demby's statement that "self-confidence is like a psychological credit card." It's true. And to my mind the best way to develop self-confidence is to know that you're operating on absolutely sound ground rules. As such, failure does not come to a person because he is not recognized by the multitudes during his lifetime or ever. Success or failure has nothing to do with the opinion of others. It has only to do with our own opinion of ourselves and confidence in what we're doing.

The only person who can be called a failure is the person who tries to succeed at nothing. Success, as far as a person is concerned, does not lie in achievement; it lies in striving, reaching, attempting. Any person who decides upon a course of action he deems to be worthy of him and sets out to accomplish that goal is a success right then and there. Therefore, failure consists not in failing to reach our goals but rather in not establishing them. Failure is not trying.

Among all living creatures, man alone is placed on earth without a built-in book of instructions for successful living. He must create his own world within the parameters of the society in which he finds himself. And he can create a good world for himself if he will become free and look for quality in everything he does, if he will learn to think, if he will examine with faint distrust everything he hears and sees and look for a better way, if he will consistently operate with integrity. In whatever field he finds himself, he will say to himself every day, "There are better ways of doing this. My job is to seek them out," and he will make as his guidelines in seeking a better way those two unfailing guideposts, quality and simplicity.

Success depends on knowing our talents and on our ability to use them to the fullest. For those who can do this, success is theirs.

NOTES

1. Bertrand Russell, *The Conquest of Happiness* (New York: Liveright, 2013), 64.

2. *Oxford English Dictionary*, 1st ed., s.v. "Character."

3. Ralph Waldo Emerson, "Fate," in *The Works of Ralph Waldo Emerson*, vol. 2 (London: George Bell and Sons, 1904), 209.

4. Konrad Lorenz, *On Aggression*, trans. Marjorie Kerr Wilson (San Diego, CA: Harvest, 1974).

5. Henry David Thoreau, *Walden* (New York: Thomas Y. Crowell & Co., 1910), 427.

6. Carl Jung quoted in Albert J. Mills et al., *Organizational Behaviour in a Global Context* (Peterborough, Ontario: Broadview Press, 2007), 217.

7. Plato, *The Dialogues of Plato*, trans. B. Jowett, 3rd ed., vol. 1 (New York: Oxford University Press, 1892), 574.

8. José Ortega y Gasset, *Some Lessons in Metaphysics*, trans. Mildred Adams (New York: Norton, 1969), 22.

9. Alan Watts, *The Nature of Man* (California: Celestial Arts, 1975).

10. Emerson, "Fate," 199.

11. Peter F. Drucker, *The Age of Discontinuity: Guidelines to Our Changing Society* (London: Butterworth-Heinemann, 1969).

12. Maslow quoted in Walter Mischel, Yuichi Shoda, and Ozlem Ayduk, eds., *Introduction to Personality: Toward an Integrative Science of the Person*, 8th ed. (Hoboken, NJ: John Wiley & Sons, 2008), 306.

13. Maslow quoted in Kirk J. Schneider, James F. T. Bugental, and J. Fraser Pierson, eds., *The Handbook of Humanistic Psychology: Leading Edges in Theory, Research, and Practice* (Thousand Oaks: Sage, 2001), 361.

14. T. H. Huxley, *Aphorisms and Reflections from the Works of T. H. Huxley*, ed. Henrietta A. Huxley (London: Macmillan, 1908), http://www.guten berg.org/files/38097/38097-h/38097-h.htm.

15. George Bernard Shaw, *Back to Methuselah*, Archive.org, http://archive .org/stream/backtomethuselah13084gut/13084.txt.

16. Proverbs 16:32 KJV.

17. William James, *Psychology: The Briefer Course* (New York: Harper & Row, 1961), 195.

18. Ibid.

19. W. MacNeile Dixon, *The Human Situation* (London: Edward Arnold, 1937), 34.

20. Northrop Frye, The Educated Imagination *and Other Writings on Critical Theory, 1933–1962*, Collected Works of Northrop Frye, vol. 21, ed. Germaine Warkentin (Toronto: University of Toronto Press, 2006), 494.

21. Ibid.

22. Emerson, "Compensation," Emerson Central, http://emersoncentral .com/texts/essays-first-series/compensation/.

23. Willard Frederick Rockwell, *The Twelve Hats of a Company President* (Upper Saddle River, NJ: Prentice-Hall, 1971).

24. Charles Erwin Wilson worked as the chief engineer and sales manager at Remy Electric, a subsidiary of General Motors, and eventually became the president of General Motors in 1941.

25. Kenneth Goode, *How to Win What You Want* (New York: Prentice-Hall, 1939).

26. Nicholas Johnson, "The Careening of America. Caution: Television Watching May Be Hazardous to Your Mental Health," in *Messages: A Reader in Human Communication*, ed. Sanford Weinberg (New York: Random House, 1980), 250–62.

27. Johnson, "Test Pattern for Living," *Saturday Review*, May 29, 1971, 12.

28. Johnson, *What Do You Mean and How Do You Know?: An Antidote for the Language That Does Our Thinking for Us* (United States: n.p., 2009), 95.

29. Russell, *Conquest*, 64.

30. Ibid.

31. Peter F. Drucker, *The Effective Executive* (New York: Harper & Row, 1967).

32. Ferdinand Lundberg, *The Rich and the Super-Rich* (New York: Lyle Stuart, 1968).

33. Scott Burns, *Squeeze It Till the Eagle Grins: How to Spend, Save, and Enjoy Your Money* (New York: Doubleday, 1972).

34. Abraham Maslow, *The Farther Reaches of Human Nature* (New York: Penguin, 1971), 35.

35. Henry James, *The Ambassadors* (Oxford: Oxford University Press, 1998), 154.

36. Emerson, "Fate," 209.

37. Matthew 6:33 KJV.

38. Huxley, "A Liberal Education," Human-Nature.com, http://human-nature.com/darwin/huxley/chap2.html.

39. Francis Bacon, *The Advancement of Learning*, Project Gutenberg, http://www.gutenberg.org/files/5500/5500-h/5500-h.htm.

40. William George Jordan, *The Majesty of Calmness: Individual Problems and Possibilities* (United States: CreateSpace, 2013), 2.

41. Arthur Schopenhauer, *The World as Will and Representation*, vol. 2, trans. E. F. J. Payne (Indian Hills, CO: The Falcon's Wing Press, 1958), 29.

42. Albert Ellis, *How to Live with a "Neurotic" at Home and at Work*, rev. ed. (United States: Wilshire Book Company, 1975).

43. Robert Louis Stevenson quoted in "Robert Louis Stevenson: An Appreciation," *The Fortnightly Review* 74 (1903): 514.

44. William Lyon Phelps, "One Day at a Time," in *A Collection of Classic Essays by William Lyon Phelps* (Worcestershire, UK: Read Books, 2013), 214.

45. Emerson, *The Complete Works*, vol. 7 (Boston: Houghton Mifflin, 1904). Bartleby.com, http://www.bartleby.com/90/0707.html.

46. Emerson, "Lecture on the Times," in *Works of Ralph Waldo Emerson in Five Volumes*, vol. 5 (Boston: Houghton, Osgood and Co., 1880). 217.

47. Ortega, *Some Lessons in Metaphysics*, 22.

48. Emerson, "Self-Reliance," Emerson Central, http://emersoncentral.com /texts/essays-first-series/self-reliance/.

49. Matthew 7:7 KJV.

50. Thoreau, *Walden*, Project Gutenberg, https://www.gutenberg.org/files /205/205-h/205-h.htm.

51. Hebrews 11:1 ESV.

52. Emerson, "Circles," The Literature Page, http://www.literaturepage.com /read/emersonessays1-158.html.

53. Ibid., http://www.literaturepage.com/read/emersonessays1-159.html.

54. Walter Kaufmann, *Without Guilt and Justice: From Decidophobia to Autonomy* (Philadelphia, PA: David McKay Co., 1973).

55. Thoreau, *Walden*, 427.

56. Harvey Mindess, *Laughter & Liberation* (Oxon, UK: Transaction Publishers, 2010), 20.

57. Mark Twain, *Notebook*, in *The Complete Works of Mark Twain* (New York: Harper & Brothers, 1923), 393.